Around the World
Single-Handed

THE ISLANDER TAKES A SAIL IN TABLE BAY.

Around the World Single-Handed

The Cruise of the "Islander"

by

Harry Pidgeon

DOVER PUBLICATIONS, INC.
NEW YORK

Published in Canada by General Publishing Company, Ltd., 30 Lesmill Road, Don Mills, Toronto, Ontario.

Published in the United Kingdom by Constable and Company, Ltd.

This Dover edition, first published in 1989, is an unabridged republication of the work originally published in 1933 by D. Appleton and Company, New York and London. The map on pp. x and xi appeared on the endpapers in the original edition.

Manufactured in the United States of America
Dover Publications, Inc., 31 East 2nd Street, Mineola, N.Y. 11501

Library of Congress Cataloging-in-Publication Data

Pidgeon, Harry.
    Around the world single-handed : the cruise of the "Islander" /
    Harry Pidgeon.
        p.   cm.
    Reprint. Originally published: New York : D. Appleton, 1933
    ISBN 0-486-25946-3
    1. Pidgeon, Harry.   2. Islander (Yawl)   3. Voyages around the world.   4. Sailing, Single-handed.   I. Title.
    G440.P63   1989
    910.4'5—dc19   88-7900
                                                                CIP

CONTENTS

ILLUSTRATIONS

vii

ILLUSTRATIONS

viii

ILLUSTRATIONS

ix

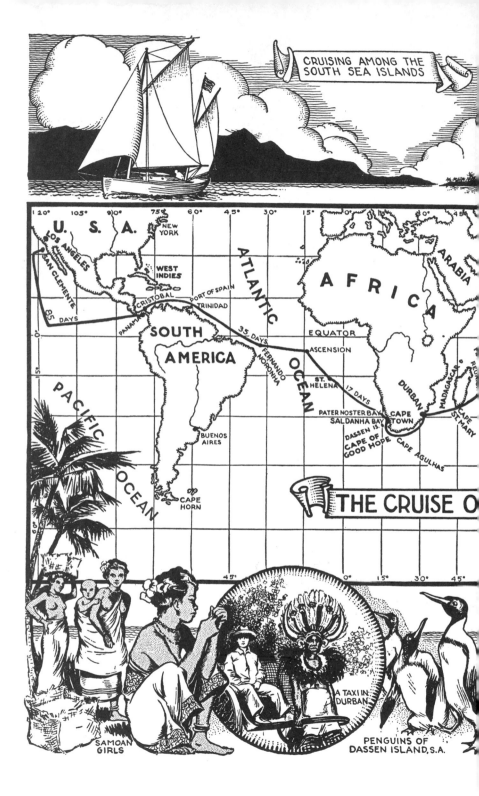

CRUISING AMONG THE
SOUTH SEA ISLANDS

U. S. A.

NEW YORK

WEST INDIES

ATLANTIC OCEAN

AFRICA

ARABIA

CRISTOBAL
PANAMA
PORT OF SPAIN
TRINIDAD

85 DAYS

SOUTH
AMERICA

35 DAYS

EQUATOR

ASCENSION

FERNANDO
NORONHA

ST.
HELENA   17 DAYS

DURBAN

MADAGASCAR

REUNION

CAPE
ST. MARY

PATER NOSTER BAY   CAPE
SALDANHA BAY   TOWN

DASSEN IS.
CAPE OF
GOOD HOPE   CAPE AGULHAS

PACIFIC OCEAN

BUENOS
AIRES

CAPE
HORN

THE CRUISE O

SAMOAN
GIRLS

A TAXI IN
DURBAN

PENGUINS OF
DASSEN ISLAND, S.A.

LOS ANGELES
SAN CLEMENTE

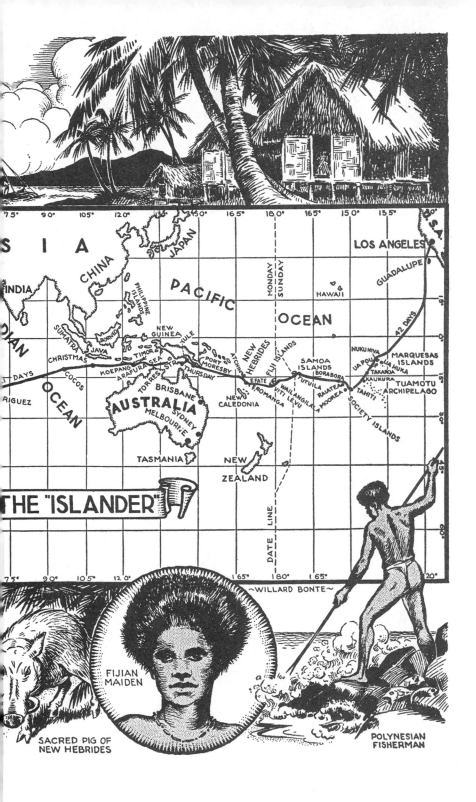

75° 90° 105° 120° 135° 150° 165° 180° 165° 150° 135°

CHINA
JAPAN
LOS ANGELES
A S I A
INDIA
PACIFIC
MONDAY
SUNDAY
HAWAII
GUADALUPE
PHILIPPINE ISLANDS
OCEAN
42 DAYS
NEW GUINEA
SUMATRA BORNEO
JAVA TIMOR
CHRISTMAS
KOEPANG
ARAFURA SEA
PORT MORESBY
ATCHIN
NEW HEBRIDES
FIJI ISLANDS
SAMOA ISLANDS
BORABORA
NUKU HIVA
UA POU UA HUKA
TAKAROA
MARQUESAS ISLANDS
...T DAYS
COCOS
TORRES STR.
THURSDAY
EFATE
EROMANGA
WAILANGILALA
VITI LEVU
TUTUILA
RAIATEA
MOOREA
KAUKURA
TAHITI
TUAMOTU ARCHIPELAGO
RIGUEZ
OCEAN
BRISBANE
AUSTRALIA
SYDNEY
MELBOURNE
NEW CALEDONIA
SOCIETY ISLANDS
TASMANIA
NEW ZEALAND
THE "ISLANDER"
DATE LINE
75° 90° 105° 120° 165° 180° 165°
~WILLARD BONTE~

FIJIAN MAIDEN

SACRED PIG OF NEW HEBRIDES

POLYNESIAN FISHERMAN

Around the World
Single-Handed

I

The Islander

THE *Islander* was my first attempt at building a sailboat, but I don't suppose there ever was an amateur built craft that so nearly fulfilled the dream of her owner, or that a landsman ever came so near to weaving a magic carpet of the sea.

As a youth I was not favorably situated for taking up a seafaring career, but I had many qualifications for the job. My love of the sea did not come from early association, for I was born on a farm in Iowa and did not see salt water until I went to California, when I was eighteen years of age. So far as I know, none of my ancestors ever followed the sea.

After some years spent on a ranch in California, I went to Alaska, where I acquired first-hand knowledge of boats. I had built a canvas canoe in California, but as I lived thirty miles from navigable water, I had not learned much about the use of it until I read Lieutenant Schwatka's, *Along the Great River of Alaska,* and decided to see that mighty stream. Another young farmer, Dan Williamson, joined me in the adventure.

Following the trail of a party of prospectors and smugglers, who had gone on before, we climbed the snowy Chilkoot Pass and built a boat on the shore of

Marsh Lake, one of the sources of the Yukon River. It was a real boat made out of boards that we whip-sawed from a spruce tree growing at hand. To propel our new craft we had made a pair of oars and a paddle.

We launched our boat off the ice into a bit of open water at the foot of the lake. I had never had a pair of oars in my hands before but I manned them now, and Dan took up the paddle. Our object was to get out of the lake and into the river that was flowing out of it, but Dan was not able to point the boat in that direction, and we only went round and round. I remembered that I had once paddled a canoe all of half a mile, so we changed about. It seems that I had the knack and Dan was strong on the oars.

We left Marsh Lake early in the morning and reached Miles Canyon the same day, after an exciting run on the swift stream, where many lives were lost during the Klondyke gold rush a few years later. At Miles Canyon we found a party of four men, who were portaging their outfits and two boats around the canyon. They volunteered to help us carry our boat over the portage; however, after taking a look at the place, I decided that we would run through, which we did the next morning. One of the party, Peter Lorent-sen, stationed himself at the lower end of the canyon to see what would happen. When we came shooting out of the gorge and rounded up to the bank where Peter was standing, he said, "Well, you boys are sailors."

2

My reply was, "If you had seen us yesterday morning, you would not have said we were sailors."

He still insisted, "I'm an old sailor, and I know that you boys are sailors."

Peter lost his life when his boat swamped as he was following close after us through the Five Finger Rapids, but we were able to save his partner, Henry, and brought him to his destination at Circle, a new mining town on the Yukon. Beyond Five Finger Rapids the Yukon was plain sailing for two farmers, who had become sailors in a day. Late that fall, from St. Michael's Island at the mouth of the river, we took passage on the little freight steamer *Bertha* for California.

I did not find it easy to settle down again after that wonderful summer on the Yukon, and I returned to Alaska, where I had many thrilling adventures on the rivers and lakes of the north. At one time I owned a small vessel and sailed it among the islands of southeastern Alaska, but I never went out upon blue water and most of my time was spent hunting and making photographs along rivers and in the mountains of that great land. The experience that I gained while building small river boats from materials growing in the woods served me well when I came to build the seagoing vessel that carried me around the world, and life in the wilds was a good school for developing resourcefulness.

While on a visit to my old home in Iowa, I remembered that it had been one of my boyhood ambitions to float down the Mississippi River to the sea. After reading an account of a houseboat journey on the river, I concluded that such a cruise might be interesting. With this idea in mind, I went to Minneapolis, and there just below the Falls of St. Anthony, built a small flatboat. I had many friends and relatives living along the river to cheer me on my way to the sea, and I learned that I could turn my photographic talent to account so as to leave a dividend at the end. For more than a year I was afloat on the river, and when I quit the little flatboat at Port Eads I had resolved to see more distant lands in a vessel of my own. From that time I began to take an interest in sailing craft and to contemplate voyages.

But it takes more than wishes to acquire a suitable craft and go on long voyages, so eventually I returned to California and became a photographer among the great trees of the Sierras. After a few years of this work, pleasant though it was, I longed for new scenes.

About this time I came across the plan of a boat that seemed to be very seaworthy and, in addition, was not too large for one man to handle. Moreover, the construction of it did not seem too difficult for my limited knowledge of shipbuilding. Business with lumbermen and tourists in the big woods, and the proceeds from the sale of a small farm, put me in possession of the necessary funds, so I decided to build my long-dreamed-of ship and go on a voyage to the isles of the sea. From the mountains I went down

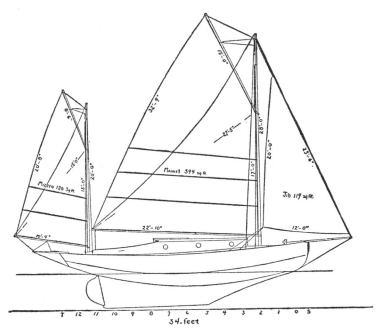

SAIL PLAN OF THE ISLANDER

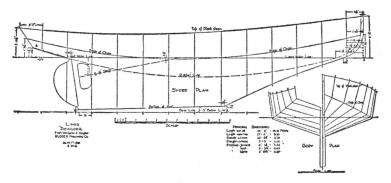

LINES OF THE ISLANDER

With permission of the Rudder Publishing Company

to the shore of Los Angeles Harbor, located on a vacant lot, and began the actual work of construction.

The plan from which I was to model my ship was one that had been drawn for Captain Thomas Fleming Day, who had had wide experience in sailing small boats, and it was Captain Day's idea of what a small seagoing craft should be. It was a V-bottom or Sea Bird boat, a type developed by Captain Day and yacht designers on the staff of the *Rudder Magazine*. The reason for using the V-bottom type was that it is easier for the amateur builder to lay down and construct. Three safe and handy cruising boats were brought out and the plans published in the *Rudder*. They were *Sea Bird*, *Naiad*, and *Seagoer*. The *Islander* was built after the lines of the *Seagoer* and the general construction plan is the same, but I used ideas from each of these boats and added some ideas of my own as suggested by the material at hand and my limited resources. All the information I had when building the *Islander* is contained in a booklet published by the Rudder Publishing Company, of New York (*How to Build a Cruising Yawl*), containing instructions for building *Sea Bird*, *Naiad*, and *Seagoer*.

With the coming in of the year 1917 the actual work of construction was commenced with the laying down of the keel. The timbers for the keel were eight by twelve inches in thickness, and the largest piece twenty-eight feet long. When I hear any one talking about my frail craft, I always think of those

6

HEWING OUT THE KEEL TIMBERS FOR THE ISLANDER.

THE ISLANDER TAKES FORM.

LAUNCHING MY NEW VESSEL IN LOS ANGELES HARBOR.

TRYING OUT THE NEW YAWL OFF CATALINA ISLAND.

keel timbers. They were cut to shape with saw and adz, and a piece of iron weighing twelve hundred and fifty pounds was cast in a near-by foundry for the bottom piece of the keel, and to act as ballast. When the timbers and iron ballast piece were bolted together with large iron bolts they formed an exceedingly strong backbone for the frame of the vessel.

Except for the stem and a few pieces about the cabin, which were of oak, the wood used in the construction was of Douglas fir or Oregon pine. The timbers for the frame were all very heavy and reënforced at the bilge with steel plates that I cut from tank plate. After the frame was bolted together as strongly as possible, the planks were put on. The bilge strake and all above were full length in one piece. Working alone, as I did, the planking was a long, hard job, and the thick, heavy boards were bent into place without the aid of a steam box. The bilge strakes were two and a half inches thick and seven and a half inches wide amidships, tapering to six inches at the ends. These pieces were bent over twenty inches edgewise as well as being brought round the curve of the sides.

After they were in place, a carpenter from a boat works looked at them and said, "I know how we would put those planks on at the shop, where we have a steam box and plenty of help, but how you got them on I can't see." It was the most difficult piece of work about the construction, but when it comes to blocking up and driving wedges they could not have beaten me in the boat shop. Those planks had to come to place or break. That they would break was what I feared, but they did not break. Gradually something like a boat began to appear, and spectators began to arrive, ask questions and give advice.

There was a beachcomber living in a shack near by, who used to come and tell me that the keel of my boat was cut away too much forward. "She won't come up into the wind. She'll fall away to loo'ard." He informed me he was going to build a boat fifty feet long and ten feet beam, in which he was going to Africa to hunt lions. He had invented a reefing gear with which he could reef sails without leaving the wheel. Was going to have an electric motor for an auxiliary and generate electricity with a windmill on deck. Nor was I the only builder on the shore. In sight of my works but across the channel on the Terminal side, a colored Moses was erecting an ark with which to transport a colony of his followers to Liberia. As he was laying down the keel, a question in regard to the size of his projected ship brought the answer that all depended on the donations he got. The donations seemed to keep coming in, for as my boat took shape, his grew into a structure two stories high, with windows alow and aloft, and a stove pipe appeared through a broken pane.

No doubt as my boat was rising from the heap of timbers on the sand it was often taken for another one of those freaks, but a yacht builder, who became interested in what I was doing, told a friend of mine that he could not do the work better himself.

When the planking was on, the deck was laid and covered with canvas and then the house was added. The sides of the house were one solid piece each, and carried aft to form the cockpit coamings. The cabin was twelve feet long, arranged with a berth on either side and spaces for drawers and a wood-burning stove. Under the deck between the house and the cockpit was a good space where supplies for a long voyage could be stored. The cockpit was built water-tight, and self-bailing through lead scuppers carried straight down through the hull.

When it came to the calking, I was advised to get a professional to do it. However, remembering the success I had had in making small boats water-tight, I approached this job with more confidence than almost any other about my new vessel, and few boats are so dry as mine.

The masts were made and fitted, and the name *Islander,* which I had given the new ship, I painted on the stern board. I dug the ground away underneath and laid down ways on which the vessel might slide into the water. Some friends, who were intending to be at the launching, thought they would have time to see a ship launched from a near-by yard and then see the *Islander* go in, but my boat went in first. From the laying down of the keel to the launching, the *Islander* came near to being entirely the work of my own hands.

9

The *Islander* was rigged as a yawl, and was thirty-four feet long over all, ten feet nine inches beam, and drew five feet of water with no load in her. She carried about six hundred and thirty square feet of sail in her three sails. She was adapted to the use of auxiliary power, but for many reasons, mostly financial, I did not install a motor. However, the real sport is to make the elements take one where he wants to go; and then a motor never functions properly when left alone with me. For a tender I built a little skiff nine feet long, and when at sea this was hauled on board, turned over against the house, and lashed fast. In this position it was carried wherever I sailed.

The *Islander* cost me about one thousand dollars for material and a year and a half of hard work.

When the sails were bent, yachting friends, who knew more about the rules of the road than I did, joined me and we tried the new ship out on a cruise to Catalina Island. She proved to sail well, and all remarked on the ease with which she handled. Many pleasant days were spent sailing about the near-by islands, sometimes with friends but more often alone, and in one of the many sunny coves in the lee of Catalina Island my little ship might be found at all seasons. In the meantime I procured books and instruments, and amid pleasant surroundings, I began to learn something of navigation.

My method of navigation was simple and consisted of determining the latitude and longitude by observation of the sun—two simple problems that require no special ability to master.

For the purposes of navigation, the earth is laid out in imaginary lines, called meridians of longitude and parallels of latitude, which may be likened to the streets and avenues of a city. The position of a ship at sea, and out of sight of land, on these meridians and parallels can be solved only by astronomical observation. When one can solve these problems he can find his way about as readily as he finds the numbers along avenues and streets of a well laid out city. Dead reckoning I kept only mentally, and that merely to keep track of my position between observations of the sun.

The textbook on navigation that I used was *Navigation*, by Harold Jacoby, but there are any number of excellent works on the subject. One must also have the *Nautical Almanac*. For navigating instruments I had two compasses, sextant, protractor, parallel ruler, dividers, and a taffrail log. For keeping the time I had two watches, one for the Greenwich mean time and one for the local time. Of course, one should have charts and sailing directions for the places where one intends to call. At times I found myself without either which was rather inconvenient.

To determine the latitude, one has only to get the declination of the sun out of the *Nautical Almanac* and then ascertain the altitude of the sun at noon with the sextant.

When the sun is between the observer and the

equator, latitude equals 90° plus the declination and minus the altitude.

With the observer between the sun and the equator, latitude equals the declination plus the altitude minus 90°.

If the observer and the sun are on opposite sides of the equator, latitude equals 90° minus the altitude minus the declination.

The principle on which the longitude is determined is simple. Calculations based on the latitude of the observer, the declination of the sun, and the altitude of the sun make known the local time at the moment of observation. At the same moment the chron‧nometer tells the Greenwich time. The difference between the two times then gives us the longitude.

For the amateur navigator, I recommend Martelli's tables when working up the time sight. With these tables the time sight is about as simple as the latitude sight, and it takes only about half as long to solve the problem as it does with the sine and cosine method given in standard works on navigation.

These problems may be solved by observation of such stars as have their position given in the *Nautical Almanac,* but in actual practice on the deck of a small vessel pitching in a seaway, I find the sun is none too large. Also under certain conditions of weather the horizon is hard to define even in broad daylight.

While the theory of navigation is simple and easy to learn, seamanship—the ability to care for and handle a vessel under all conditions and stresses of weather—is acquired only by experience and long practice. When I felt myself competent, I set about preparations for an overseas voyage.

"Why did you do it?" is the question that I am most often asked in regard to my sailing alone. One of the best reasons I had was the lack of means with which to buy a larger vessel and hire a crew to sail it for me. There is also a great satisfaction in accomplishing something by one's own effort. Men have often said to me, "That is what I have always dreamed of doing, but you have done it." During my long voyage I met several parties that were seeing the world from the decks of beautiful yachts, surrounded by friends, and the luxuries that wealth will buy; but none of them seemed to be getting the thrill of joy out of it that I was in my little yawl.

When I was preparing to set out alone across the ocean for the first time I had something of a fellow feeling for those ancient mariners who believed that there was an abyss into which all ships would sail if they ventured into the unknown beyond the horizon. Then a little incident occurred that removed all doubt in my mind as to the question of sailing alone.

My friend W——, who had a yacht somewhat larger than mine, decided to break the monotony of the racing game with a cruise to the Hawaiian Islands. After enlisting two landsmen in the venture, it occurred to him that I would be a desirable addition to the expedition. With a view to getting valuable sea experience before going it alone I gave the *Islander* in charge of a friend and took my kit aboard the outbound yacht. We sailed in the gray of the morning, as befitted a crew of sea rovers. Among other stores in the galley was a box of plums that one of our shipmates had brought from his fruit ranch up country. Inspection showed the plums to be in an advanced stage of ripeness, so it was decided to eat them at once. When clear of the land we ran into a brave southwest wind, blowing about thirty-five miles an hour and kicking up a nasty sea. The yawl plowed through the billows nobly, tossing up clouds of foam and spray that drenched everything aboveboard and ran in a stream through the skylight into the cabin. The hastily eaten plums soon found their way into the scuppers, but all day long the yawl did her nine knots an hour on the course. As evening came on I clung to the tiller, wet and shivering, resigned to a prospect of standing an all-night watch. The skipper was below consulting with our now disabled seamen, who had taken to their berths. In the gathering gloom of dusk he came up and announced, "This is going to be a wet, nasty trip, and I am going back." I started to remonstrate, but it was no use. The morale of the crew was low, he said. He had had enough of the deep-sea stuff, and did not think it would be wise to go on. Perhaps he was right. We sailed out all day and then sailed back all night.

I returned to the *Islander* with a feeling that the problems of a single-handed sailor were comparatively simple.

II

A Voyage to Hawaii

MY first ocean voyage in the *Islander* was to Hawaii. It was the greatest adventure of my life when I sailed alone with my new ship into what was, to me, an unknown region, and for the first time to put to practical use the theories of navigation that I had lately acquired.

The day could not have been fairer. Boats large and small were hurrying in and out on errands of business or pleasure, and among them the *Islander* glided on her way and stood out to sea. Out of the calm under the lee of San Clemente Island she ran into the old familiar southwest wind that had so disheartened my companions on that earlier attempt at a deep-sea voyage.

When discussing the question of single-handed sailing, I am continually being asked, "What do you do at night?" That was what I now began to learn for myself, and I lost a lot of sleep while doing it.

Off the California coast the southwest wind was ahead of the beam, and the *Islander* held the course well, but I did not feel like sleeping and spent most of the first night at sea crouched in the cockpit sheltering myself the best I could from wind and spray. The wind abated somewhat, and on the second night my little yawl, under shortened sail, sailed serenely on while I slept. On the evening of the fifth day out, the wind came round to the north and blew hard with a rough sea. I tied the third reef in the mainsail and stowed the mizzen, and all night long I sat at the tiller, keeping off when a white roller came up abeam. My eyes were tired with watching the compass, but when I dozed off for a moment I would be roused up by a sea breaking over and drenching me with cold water. But the night wore away, and the gale went down. With the rising sun the dark storm clouds of the night broke into fleecy masses that drifted on and on until they passed beyond the horizon. Where the sunlight broke through and fell on the sea the water was bluer than any I had ever seen, and a blue haze seemed to float over the surface. I had picked up the northeast trade winds. Once in the trades I was running almost before the wind, and it required close attention to keep the little yawl on the course with all sails set. Finding that I was wearing myself out I began to take things easier, and when the weather was boisterous I stowed the main and mizzen sails at night, and let the *Islander* run on under the jib. Even then the shivering of the jib at the leech was enough to keep me awake. In the end I learned to shorten sail and get it balanced, so that the *Islander* would sail on almost any course while I slept. If she did run off the course a bit, what of it?

One night, during a squall, the jib halyard parted

and let the jib come down. When the weather moderated the next day, I rigged up a boatswain's chair on the peak halyard with which to go up and reeve in a new one. The motion at the masthead was so violent that it required all my strength to keep from being shaken off. After great exertion I managed to get the job done and was glad to get down on deck again with nothing worse than a few bruises. Ever afterwards, when I have been getting ready for going to sea, I have seen to it that the halyards and all aloft were in good order.

The method that I used in finding my way about on the sea was the simplest imaginable. When I was taking my departure from San Clemente Island, I put out a new log, but it soon ceased to register, and I never did get the thing to work. This little incident eliminated any work that might have been attached to keeping track of my position by dead reckoning. The motion of a small vessel in a seaway is quick, if not actually violent. While the motion of the *Islander* did not interfere with my working ship or standing watch at the tiller it was very different when I went below and attempted to solve a problem in mathematics. The very first time that I opened the tables and started to work a time sight, something began to gyrate in my head and I realized that I was not immune to seasickness. I closed the old tome and did not work a time sight problem on the run. My method was to estimate the time as near as possible when taking the noon sight for latitude, and from this time

17

get the approximate longitude. As I was intending to make my landfall on the latitude, this seemed to be sufficiently accurate.

I like company as well as any one, but in my wanderings I had already learned to go it alone so I was not fretting about the loneliness of the voyage. My chief worry was carrying sail at night and getting enough sleep at the same time. As I was passing into a new clime there was usually something of interest to attract my attention during the daylight hours.

At noon on the thirteenth day out, when I threw up my sextant for a sight, I found that I had passed under the sun and for the first time I was to the south of it. On the same day a beautiful white tropic bird, the first I had ever seen, paid the *Islander* a visit, and I began to realize that I was in the tropics at last.

One squally evening I stowed the mainsail and left the *Islander* to find her own way through the night. After I had eaten my evening meal, and before I lay down, I went up to take a look around. I was not looking for land, and according to my reckoning it was a long way off, but I was not so sure about my navigation. A peculiar dark cloud loomed up ahead and fragments of white clouds went driving over it, giving it the appearance of a mountain. As I sat watching, a light twinkled and it all appeared so real that I sprang to loose the mainsail with which to stand off a lee shore. When I went into action, the light disappeared and the cloud began to break up. For a time I stared into the darkness and then turned into my berth to finish my dream.

The only vessel sighted on the passage was a large four-masted schooner, her deck piled high with lumber. She was in sight all day and slowly forged ahead of my little ship until she made a grand picture outlined against the golden glow of sunset. I made no doubt that her destination was the Hawaiian Islands and was more confident of my own navigation. The next day I saw great numbers of birds and began to watch for the appearance of land.

On the twenty-fifth day out I calculated my position to be north of the Island of Hawaii, but heavy clouds obscured the horizon. Late in the afternoon I sighted a dark object high among the clouds. It remained stationary and was in sight for about an hour before the clouds closed over it once more. It was land, and probably the summit of Haleakala on Maui Island. During the night the *Islander* drifted on under the jib, and with the coming of daylight I saw land on the port beam, where, below the low-lying clouds, the deeply furrowed side of an island sloped down to the sea, but there was not enough visible for me to recognize it. In the evening I came up to Oahu but mistook it for Molokai until I saw the flash of the light on Makupuu Head.

I came up off Honolulu Harbor at midnight and lay off and on till morning watching the twinkling lights of the city. I was tired and sleepy, and during my twenty-six days alone on the sea I had lost much of my enthusiasm for single-handed sailing. With the coming of daylight, I took a good look at the place, for the long beat back to California against the trade wind did not seem alluring, and I thought this was going to be my home for a long time.

There was a fragrance in the breeze that came drifting out from the land. I was sea weary and so soon as the channel through the reef could be made out I sailed in, but I did not go on shore that day. First I had a discussion with the grizzled health officer, who seemed to think I should have stayed outside until he had given me permission to come in. As soon as the anchor was down visitors began to arrive. At the first opportunity I lay down for a few minutes' rest. It was nine o'clock that night before I awoke, and it was near two weeks before I had caught up on sleep.

It was my first visit to a tropical isle, and it seemed all the more wonderful to me coming, as I did, from my first long lonesome voyage at sea. I found friends on the island, and the time passed pleasantly whether it was spent hiking on the mountains or sitting in the shade along the shore. These splendid islands attract many notable visitors. While the *Islander* was resting in Honolulu Harbor, the British cruiser, *Renown,* came in with the Prince of Wales on board, so they had the two of us there at the same time.

My memory seems to retain pleasant impressions better than it does unpleasant ones. When recounting my voyage, after coming on shore, it appears that I had not had such a disagreeable time after all, and when a few of my new acquaintances had extended their compliments, I was in a frame of mind to try it again.

Of the scenic places on the island, there was one that attracted me more than any other. It was the Pali, against which the trade winds banked and surged. At one time while I was at this romantic spot, a rain storm swept over the heights, and from a gulch in a near-by cliff, a good-sized stream poured forth. The wind sweeping up the perpendicular rock wall, caught the stream as it left the gulch and carried it up and up until it was blown to a mist, and one beheld a waterfall going up instead of coming down. It was this wind that I had run before on my way to Hawaii, and against it I would have to contend on my way back to California.

Among new acquaintances in Honolulu was a young man from California, Earl Brooks, who often accompanied me on sight-seeing tours about the island. When I was making preparations for the return voyage, he proposed going with me. As his nautical experience had been limited to washing dishes on the *Matsonia* while outward bound from California, there seemed to be no danger of his wanting to take charge of the ship, so I took him on as mate.

During the time the *Islander* lay in Honolulu Harbor a coral crust had grown on her bottom. A day was spent scraping it off. We rove in new running rigging, and as there was a possibility of running into rough weather, I made a sea anchor out of some boards. We put on ample supplies of food and water for many days, and Mr. Brooks bought a new guitar. When he came on board with his new acquisition, I asked him what he was going to do with it, and he said he was going to while away the time learning to play on it. Thinking of the thousands of miles of head winds we were going to contend with, I concluded that he did not know what he was running into. Well, he was not much of a musician when the voyage was done.

We sailed from Honolulu on the morning of September 23rd. The trade wind was blowing strong when we rounded the island and stood into it on a course north by east under close reefed sails. With the coming of night the happy isle faded from our sight, and out of the darkness frequent squalls swept down on us.

When we were clear of the land we set watches of four hours each and carried on day and night. The sea was rough enough at the start to affect the appetites of the crew, but the mate's stomach gave way in a good old-fashioned style that relieved him somewhat, and he stuck to his watch gamely enough.

We had taken on a large bunch of bananas when sailing from Honolulu, but I was not able to eat the lot myself. Thinking that the mate's appetite for bananas might improve later on, I tried preserving some of them in a Mason jar. I packed the jar full of the ripe fruit, screwed on the lid and set it in a pot of boiling water. I was busy with something else when the lid blew off with a startling report. For a moment I thought the ship's magazine had blown up, and the whole interior of the cabin, including myself, was plastered with the sticky mess. For some reason the spectacle seemed to cheer the mate's spirits wonderfully.

On the third day out we built a fire and cooked a meal with vegetable soup, rice, flying fish and toast on the menu.

As it was impracticable for a small sailboat to beat back to California against the trade wind, our object was to stand to the northward until we were out of it. A course north by east was held until September 27th, when in latitude 28° north we ran out of the trade winds. On the evening of that day the wind died out and we were becalmed. The next morning a light breeze sprung up out of the south and gradually came round to the southwest. In the evening a fierce squall, the forerunner of a gale, struck us out of the northeast. We soon had sail reduced to the reefed mizzen and put out the sea anchor, and for thirty-six hours we lay drifting off to southwest. The wind then came round to east, and for another thirty-six hours we ran off to the north under shortened sail. At the end of that time we ran out of the storm as suddenly as we ran into it.

We were now in the region of variable winds north of the trades, and made our way to east by north as best we could. At times we were becalmed and went for a swim around the boat, and at other times we lay hove to in a head gale. We soon found that the *Islander* would heave to under storm jib and reefed mizzen and be more comfortable than when riding to the sea anchor. Occasionally we had a day of sunshine when we could dry our wet garments, and Brooks would bring out his guitar and cheer us with a song. In our little world every floating object that appeared to have once been connected with the land caused some excitement. Once when we were becalmed our curiosity was aroused by an object in the sea, and I swam off and brought in a cake of some waxy substance weighing about fifteen pounds, but we were not chemists enough to tell what it was. Twice we saw lights passing in the night, and all hands came on deck to watch till they disappeared, but no vessels were sighted in daylight.

Our highest latitude was 36° north. We would find more westerly winds farther north, but already the nights seemed cold to us, just from the tropics. Brooks was beginning to dread his watch from eight o'clock to midnight, which he called the graveyard watch, though I always took the watch from midnight to four o'clock. Like myself, Brooks had been an outdoor lad and our conversations often turned to camp life in the Sierras, where our experiences had been similar. And now on this vast expanse of water, when night was coming on dark and gloomy and the cold salt spray was drenching the man at the tiller,

Brooks would look at me, pathetic-like, and say, "Oh, let's go into camp."

We had several days of light changeable winds and at the same time a long heavy swell came rolling down from the north. My conclusion was that there was a severe storm raging over the Pacific farther north, and we were content to be where we were. Shortly after midnight on October 27th, the wind shifted from southwest to north by west and rose to a gale in a succession of squalls. But it was a favorable wind for us and we made the best run of the voyage. The full moon was flooding the billows with light while the *Islander* dashed in and out of the cloud shadows and over the foaming seas. Then sitting on deck amid drifting spray, we saw, between flying cloud fragments, the moon pass through the shadow in a total eclipse. I had never witnessed an eclipse amid a setting so wild, and it made a deeper impression on my mind than any similar phenomenon before or since.

The wind increased and came round to north by east, while we took in sail till only the mizzen and storm jib were left. Ever under this short sail the *Islander* moved slowly to eastward. During this storm we estimated that the crests of the seas were more than twenty feet above the trough, but our little ship rode them buoyantly, while we rested below, only taking a look out occasionally to see if all was well. To a farmer and an undertaker's son it was a wonderful experience.

By October 31st, the gale had blown itself out and

the sea was going down. We put on sail and shook out reef after reef. The next day, under full sail, we ran into greenish tinted water and the sea was covered with drifting kelp that had been torn loose in a gale that had swept the northwest coast a few days earlier.

From an observation of the sun at noon on November 2nd, I made out our position to be latitude 33°08′, longitude 120° west and laid a course to pass the southeast end of San Nicholas Island. We kept a close watch through the night and early the next morning the sand dunes of San Nicholas lay close at hand on the port beam. So much for my second-hand watch and rough method of navigation. The landfall could not have been closer with cross bearings from two stars. It seemed strange that we moved at all in the calm that followed, but two days later the anchor was dropped in an old familiar cove at Catalina Island. Forty-three days from land to land, our clothes white and stiff with salt but never feeling better, and what is remarkable there had been no trouble between ourselves.

I have read with interest the accounts of several amateur sailors, who dwelt at length on how the land seemed to heave under them when going on shore after a long passage. It seems that Brooks and I had gotten over this amateur stage of the game, for when we struck out over the Catalina hills we were as much at home as two goats.

III

Off for the South Seas

I LEARNED something of the sea on the voyage to Hawaii and became acquainted with the *Islander;* for ships, like men, have a personality of their own. My ship had become something more than just a fair-weather craft, and I had found the sea to be a great highway leading to wherever I wished to go. Confidence had come with experience, and I began preparations for a voyage to the South Seas.

Such changes as experience suggested were made in the rigging of the *Islander;* parts were renewed or strengthened where they were weak. I made a sea anchor out of canvas, and still having time on my hands, I made a new suit of sails. My friend, W—, who had given up the deep-sea idea, gave me his compass, which was larger than mine, and a taffrail log that would run. Charts and sailing directions were procured for the Marquesas, Society Islands, and Samoa, which places I intended to visit before returning to California. At the same time I had it in mind to extend the voyage if circumstances were favorable.

When it came to provisioning ship my wants were simple. There was ample space for supplies; and of staples that would keep, such as beans, peas, rice, dried

27

fruits, sugar, and bacon, I laid in a sufficient supply to last several months. For bread I carried wheat and corn, which I ground in a small hand mill as needed. These were stored in tightly closed containers that excluded moisture and insects. Of tinned goods I had salmon, milk, and fruits, but the can opener never occupied a conspicuous place in the *Islander's* galley.

I took along only what potatoes, onions, and fresh vegetables could be used before spoiling and renewed the supply at every opportunity. I always used whatever native fruits and vegetables could be obtained at the places I visited. Of water I had carrying capacity for about one hundred gallons. I can get along very well on half a gallon per day. At sea I used salt water for bathing purposes. I never failed to get results from my wood-burning stove. I have yet to come into port hungry, and my health was good at the end of the longest runs.

Sailing alone out on the great ocean is not a very cheerful prospect, and I contemplated taking along one of my acquaintances, of whom a number seemed to want to accompany me, but nothing came of it. After the return of the *Islander* from Hawaii, my mate Brooks had gone to San Francisco where he joined with three other adventurers in the purchase of a small ketch which they fitted out for a trading and treasure hunting expedition along the south coast. Dissension had already broken out among the crew when the *Los Amigos* arrived at Los Angeles Harbor.

As a consequence Brooks came ashore. We talked over the matter of his joining me, but memories of his experience on board the *Los Amigos* and of the graveyard watch on the *Islander* caused him finally to decide for a career on shore. So I went single-handed, and when once under way I was glad of it, for it was only the starting that was hard.

At noon on November 18, 1921, I sailed from Los Angeles for the Marquesas Islands. A fair wind was blowing and I sailed south rapidly enough to escape a storm that broke soon after my departure. At a later date I learned that the worst gale in years had swept the California coast, and there was much speculation as to whether my little craft would ride it out, but I had already passed out of the storm area.

On the morning of the third day out I was surprised to see the sun rising over some blue mountain peaks rising high on the eastern horizon. It was Guadalupe Island but I had not realized that it was so high or that my course would take me in sight of it. It looked mysterious, and I wondered if any one lived there. But the island quickly disappeared in the clouds that were gathering, and the north wind was sweeping me onward.

For several days I ran right before the wind with the sails gybing occasionally. Once, when I did not duck my head low enough, one of the reefing cleats caught me behind the ear. I fell on my hands and knees in the cockpit and for a moment forgot where I was.

Down about latitude 17° north a gale sprang up, and at nightfall I took off the main and mizzen sails, put on the storm jib and hauled it flat amidships. Then, with the tiller lashed amidships, the *Islander* drove off before it, requiring no attention, and there was no fear of her broaching to. It might be said that she was hove to stern first, but with the wind from the north she was still going south two or three knots an hour. The sea was a seething white waste, and the motion was violent, so I did not sleep well. As I stood at the companionway watching the surges go by, one of them would occasionally boil over the stern and pour into the cockpit. The worst of the gale had blown out by morning, and I put on the close reefed mainsail. All day we drove on over the tumbling seas till dusk when I was glad to leave the *Islander* to find her own way under the storm jib, while I went below to find refreshments and rest. There may have been much lost sleep, but the weather was never so bad that I could not cook a meal over my wood stove. It was the third day before the storm subsided and I shook out the reefs.

On the evening of that day, in latitude 11° north, I saw lightning flashing in the south, indicating the doldrums. Ahead of me the next morning two great black clouds formed, one on either hand. They rose to enormous height and spread out till they met above, and I sailed right into what appeared to be a vast tunnel between them. The rain fell in torrents, and at midday it was dark as dusk. At intervals fierce

30

squalls came shrieking along, when I lowered all sail and the *Islander* ran off before the blast doing about six knots under bare poles. Late in the afternoon I saw light ahead and ran out of the storm.

I was entering the doldrums: the region of storms and calms. Sometimes there was sunshine, then again it rained the day through. I filled my empty water bottles, and I could have caught water for the voyage in a single downpour. There were gusts of wind springing up from every quarter, and there was a squall in sight most of the time. A fair wind would breeze up only to die out, leaving my craft tossing in the cross seas. While endeavoring by all means to go south, there was one day when I gained only one minute of latitude, the equivalent of one mile, in twenty-four hours. I had little sleep, for I was on the alert day and night to catch any stray puffs of wind that came my way.

The scenery up in cloudland was wonderful, and often I had a school of fishes or porpoises for company. One lone dolphin played around my boat for two days, and seemed to be watching me when I leaned over the side. Once I went swimming with the dolphin around my ship. The *Islander* with all sails set looked strange and large when I swam off to one side so as to get a better view, and as she rose and fell on the waves, she seemed to be gliding away, and I thought how lonesome I would be if she went off and left me alone on the sea. There was an almost irresistible impulse to rush to her side and climb on board, though there was no wind and the sails and tiller were set to bring her up into the wind if it blew.

But the wind did blow once in a while, else I should be in the doldrums yet. One night the wind came up fair, when the sea was so phosphorescent that I could see the light from the water thrown off the bow flash on the sails. The next morning a gale was blowing from the southeast. In two days it had settled down to a steady breeze from east by south. I had met the southeast trade wind in latitude 5° north. During the forenoon of December 21st, in longitude 129° west I crossed the equator. It was my first time, but no special ceremony was held on board. The monotony of the run down the southeast trades was broken now and then by the appearance of some bird or sea creature that was new to me. I saw for the first time the man-of-war bird, whose picture I was familiar with in old prints of the sea. One day there appeared ahead what seemed to be a patch of floating kelp. When alongside I made out the head and flippers of an enormous turtle of startling proportions in the midst of a mass of sea weed that was clinging to it. The thing was most likely harmless, but I did not stop to molest it.

With most sea creatures the main object of life appears to be to eat or be eaten, but the porpoises often seemed to be gamboling about for the joy of it. Schools of porpoises would often play about the *Islander* until I began to distinguish individuals from their fellows by some peculiar markings or scars. One of these would leap vertically high in the air and spin around like a top.

At last, according to my reckoning, I was in the neighborhood of the Marquesas Islands. Great numbers of birds were seen, and I began to watch for the appearance of land. Up to the time of sailing into the doldrums, I had made such good time that I was beginning to look forward to making the passage of some three thousand miles in thirty days. But what with the two weeks in the doldrums and the light winds south of the line, the voyage had lengthened out until I was going to appreciate the land when I set foot on it once more.

The morning of December 30th was cloudy. I was up at half past three o'clock but could see only clouds on the horizon. The *Islander* was sailing along under the jib and mizzen sail, doing three or four knots. I went to sleep again and awoke at dawn. Springing up quickly, I looked out, and there right ahead, seeming very close, lay Uahuka Island with its green peak rising into a veil of clouds. I ran close by the south side of the island and saw houses under the trees, but the inmates were not stirring. Sailing on I passed two small islets, the home of innumerable birds that flew in a cloud over the surrounding sea. After drifting out of a calm under the lee of Uahuka, I stood away to where Nukahiva lay dimly outlined in clouds and mist. Out in the channel the wind came strong and squally. I lowered the mainsail and tied in the second reef. Before putting it on again, I cooked my breakfast and shaved the stubble of the voyage from my face.

I had read so much of Nukahiva and so long had I pored over the chart and sailing directions, that it seemed like turning over the pages of a familiar book as headlands and bays opened out to view. The wind blew strong and the sea was running high when I came up off Cape Martin. A squall swept out of Comptroller Bay, but the *Islander,* under her shortened sail, drove on before it. Then came the two Sentinel Rocks with Taiohae Bay opening out between them. Standing in, I ran under the lee of the land, and began beating up to the anchorage with the gusts of wind that came down from the lofty mountains, first from one hand and then the other. I could see houses on the shore, and smoke rising from among the trees, and knew that the place was inhabited, and I was joyous with the knowing that I was to break my solitude and meet fellow beings. When the sun was low over the peaks of Nukahiva, I dropped anchor off the beach at Taiohae, after forty-two days at sea, during which time there was never the sight of a sail or the smoke of a passing steamer.

André Alexander, the French commissioner, came off and after he learned that I came from California, welcomed me with, "Come on shore and have dinner with me. I lived in San Francisco four years."

I went on shore where a group of residents had gathered and were discussing the mysterious stranger who had arrived all alone. Bob McKittrick, the local storekeeper, translated some of this native wit for my benefit. One of them said, "He did start with some one, but he killed him on the way."

IV

The Marquesas Islands

THE *Islander* never sailed into a fairer haven than the Bay of Taiohae. After passing through the entrance, about half a mile wide, a beautiful basin, about a mile and a half in diameter, opens out. From the fringe of coconut trees on the shore, the land slopes upward in many glens and valleys to the crags of the mountain range that surrounds the bay on all sides except at the entrance on the south side.

No island of the sea has attracted me as this one has—not alone for the grandeur of its scenery, but for its romantic history as well. During the War of 1812 Captain David Porter, of the United States frigate *Essex,* took possession of Nukahiva and used Taiohae Bay as his base. And here Melville deserted the whaler to wander with Toby into the Vale of Typee.

Coming after so long a voyage alone on my little ship to this island of my dreams, it seemed the most romantic place in the world.

When discovered, the islands were densely populated, but with the coming of the white man, epidemic after epidemic swept the inhabitants off until at the time of my visit less than two thousand remained.

Scattered here and there in the shade of coconut and breadfruit trees were the houses of less than one hundred people who lived on the shore of this magnificent bay, and few of these were pure Marquesans.

Amid beautiful scenery and a healthy climate, they lived surrounded by their pigs, chickens, and dogs, and with mangoes, papayas, and bananas growing in profusion all around. Never have I seen a place where tropical produce flourished more luxuriantly or grew with less care.

After carrying on alone at sea for six weeks it seemed good to have the *Islander* anchored in a quiet harbor, and I was tired enough to enjoy the luxury of an all-night sleep without having to turn out every hour or so to see if all was well or to look for land ahead. That with a swim in the early morning and I was feeling fit as ever.

Bob McKittrick, the storekeeper, was not long in making his appearance, bringing me a pail of avocado pears, avocas, he called them, and they were better ones than I had seen elsewhere.

Bob hailed from Liverpool, was a seaman, and had been everywhere, including California. Out of the lot he had chosen Taiohae for a permanent mooring. He was greatly interested in sailboats and gave me an account of two English yachts, the *Amarillas,* and *Dream Ship,* whose wanderings had brought them to Taiohae recently. When Bob had looked over the *Islander* and gotten her record, we repaired to the shore and he went to show me the way to the mineral spring.

The spring was about a mile from the landing, and the road led through the village and by the side of a brook that meandered down a glen to the sea. From under some large stones in the shade of a mango tree a small clear stream poured out. What properties the water had no one seemed to know, but it was charged with gas and was reputed to be very wholesome. It was preferable to the water of the brook, and the mangoes were of delicious flavor, so I had occasion to visit the spring often.

On the way back from the spring we stopped at the house of Repoy. He had seen us pass as we were going up, and was waiting to insist on our giving him a call. He opened green coconuts and set out some fruit for our refreshment, and then questioned me at length, Bob acting as interpreter. Excepting some individuals of mixed breed, Repoy said he was the sole survivor of the once numerous Happar tribe. He had taken a wife of Taiohae, and had come there to live. Although Bob ridiculed him, Repoy insisted that he had once been a sailor, and my coming from America alone was no end of wonderment to him. The visit of a stranger was an important incident breaking into the monotony of their simple lives, and we left the old couple with their heads together prattling like two excited children.

Soon after my first visit to the mineral spring, an old fisherman with a shriveled arm paddled alongside

TAIOHAE BAY

Forty-two days out from Los Angeles, I sailed into these quiet waters of Nukahiva Island.

CALLING ON REPOY, THE LAST OF THE HAPPERS.

TAIOA BAY, HARBOR FOR HAKAUI VALLEY, WITH THE ISLANDER
AT ANCHOR.

HOME OF TAHIA O KAHE, IN HAKAUI VALLEY.

in a curious outrigger canoe. He divided with me a large fish he had just caught, and came on board to exchange ideas. In the few words that we had in common, we managed to talk about boats, fish, and a little gossip. He said he was a Tahitian, and like Repoy, the Happar, he had been a sailor and one of his voyages had been to Port Townsend, Washington, where he said he had met one of his own countrymen, who was married to an American Indian woman. He had, so he told me, been thrown from a horse when a young man and his shoulder had been dislocated. It had never been set, and he was going through life with his right arm almost useless. Thus my acquaintance with Tapi Moe began, and during my stay at Taiohae, he saw to it that my pots never went empty for want of native produce. If he caught but two fish he gave me one, though a crowd stood on the beach waiting to buy. Between Repoy and Tapi there was rivalry as to who should furnish me with breadfruit and bananas.

Tapi's house stood in a coconut grove on the opposite side of the brook from the home of Repoy, and he lived alone, for he was a widower. A path branched off the main road, crossed the brook to Tapi's place, and then rejoined the road near the mineral spring. I made frequent excursions to the spring for the purpose of refilling my water bottle, and whichever way I went up, I must return the same way. If I passed Repoy's house on the way to the spring, then when I returned, he would be waiting for me with breadfruit or bananas. If I took the side path through the coconut grove by Tapi's humble dwelling, there was sure to be a basket full of something set out on his *pai-pai* when I returned. Toward the end of my stay, when fresh breadfruit was scarce, I remonstrated with Tapi, saying, "You have none left for yourself," but he said, "Me got plenty *taro*," and insisted that I take it.

It was two weeks after my arrival before another vessel disturbed the waters of Taiohae Bay; then the schooner *Hinano* from Tahiti came in. Her skipper, Captain Vio, was a native of the Tuamotus. He gave me a call, but his English was only a shade better than my French so our conversation was not extensive. He looked over the *Islander* with much interest, and copied some of the elements out of my *Nautical Almanac*, saying that his almanac was for the year 1918. And the *Hinano* was the mail boat.

Arriving on the *Hinano* was M. Tissot, a Swiss, who was interested in the *Islander* for a different reason. He was a trader residing on Uapu Island, and was looking for a way to cross over to his home.

Looking out from Taiohae on a clear day the blue outline of an island, lying some thirty miles south of Nukahiva, could be seen. Its name, Uapu, signifies "The Island of Night." While Tissot was inquiring about a boat to take him over to Uapu, it was found that there were others who wanted to go. From the first time that I caught sight of its spirelike peaks, the isle had attracted me, so I invited the party to come on board for an excursion. There were Tissot, Mr. and Mrs. Sterling, American missionaries, Commissioner Alexander and his housekeeper.

The southeast trade wind was blowing strong, and once out of the bay we drove into a procession of white-capped billows that drenched us continuously with clouds of spray. It was too hot to stay in the shelter of the cabin, but no one seemed to mind the water pouring over them. Most of my passengers were seasick, but five hours brought us to our destination in Hakahetau Bay. We came up the bay so quickly that the people watching from the shore thought we were using a motor, and Tissot was so well pleased with the way the *Islander* sailed that he was offering to buy her. The usual run of boats among the islands were not much going to windward under sail.

Hakahetau Bay is not so well sheltered as Taiohae Bay, but a ledge of rock extends out beyond the breakers forming a natural mole on which my passengers were landed from the deep outrigger canoe of a native, who came out for them. The surf was breaking on a steep boulder beach, and I was fortunate to land dry when I later went on shore in my dinghy. When I was ready to go on board again, the natives carried my dinghy to the end of the rock ledge. There it was balanced over the edge, and when I was seated with oars ready, they launched me off on the top of an incoming swell.

To me, every island seems to have some characteristic differing from all other islands. The distinguishing feature of Uapu was the spirelike peaks that rise above its verdure-clad ridges and pierce far into the trade wind clouds. Almost always shrouded in mist, they occasionally stand out with startling distinctness through the rifts in the clouds.

On my last day at the island I brought my lantern ashore and entertained the people of the village with pictures of other lands that I had visited. As it was late when the gathering broke up, Tissot insisted on my staying on shore for the night. I awoke during the night and remembered that I had not wound my watches on board. I went to the landing and found the wind coming out of the northeast and driving into the bay a heavy swell that was breaking with violence on the shore. The sea was washing right over the ledge at the landing so that did not seem a likely place from which to launch my dinghy. I turned to the beach. The shore was steep and the swells did not break until they were close in; then they fell with such force as to clash the boulders about. I pushed the dinghy out as far as I could without swamping it in the breakers and stood holding it bow on to the incoming seas. Then when a big one had flung its white crest on the shore till I was near waist deep in the flood, I gave the dinghy a heave, scrambled in, and with a few quick strong pulls at the oars mounted the incoming sea just in time to keep from being upended and smashed on the stony beach. A little sleep was lost but the Greenwich time was saved.

I was intending to go on shore the next morning, but the returning party was brought off in an outrigger canoe. These native-made crafts are about the best surf boats that I have yet seen. They are built somewhat like a fishing dory, but with the flat, narrow bottom fashioned out of a log of hard wood that is not injured when landing on the rocks. The clincher-built sides are very high, so the canoe is not easily swamped in the surf. Like all outrigger boats, either end is bow or stern according to which way it is going.

When we were outside of Hakahetau Bay the wind dropped to a light breeze, and close-hauled into it a strong current set us down toward the west end of Nukahiva. A large four-masted schooner that apparently was trying to get into Taiohae Bay also drifted down to leeward, and though making every effort to beat to windward fell away altogether and disappeared to westward of Uapu. We ran close in by the shore of Nukahiva just off Taioa Bay, where the current was not so strong and we were able to make headway against it.

Emptying into Taioa Bay is a small stream that flows down to it through a valley hemmed in by a scene of grandeur that is remarkable even among these islands where scenic wonders are commonplace. As seen through the narrow, rockbound entrance, the bay did not look like an inviting place to sail into, but my companions assured me that, inside, an arm of the bay turned off at an angle and formed a landlocked cove. As we sailed along viewing the fantastic cliffs from the sea, Taioa Bay headed the list of places that I intended to see more of.

Beating up along the shore of the island, we reached Taiohae at sunset, but it was about two weeks before the schooner showed up again. It turned out to be the *Rosamond,* of San Francisco, coming to Taiohae for a load of copra. When she fell to leeward on her first attempt to get into port she stood off to southward looking for a region where there was less current, and must have sailed more than a thousand miles before she was able to get to windward once more.

I was showing some views of California to the people at Taiohae, and threw a picture of Yosemite Valley on the screen. A native promptly called out, "Hakaui." Hakaui is the wonderful valley extending inland from Taioa Bay. A few days after my return from Uapu, I sailed around to see this Yosemite of the Marquesas. The wind blew fair into the entrance of the bay, but inside, it was so completely cut off that I had to take to the sweep to get into the cove that opened out to the right. Taioa Bay is, in shape, like a shoe, with the stream from Hakaui Valley flowing in at the heel, and the white sand beach at the head of the cove is in the toe.

When the *Islander* was anchored in the quiet cove, I set out to walk to the village in Hakaui Valley where Mrs. Sterling had asked me to deliver a parcel to her friend, Louise Tamarii. I inquired of a young man whom I met on the road the way to the Tamariis' house.

After reading the address, he understood and indicated that he would go with me, but first he scaled a tall coconut tree for some green nuts, which he opened for my benefit. There is nothing more refreshing on a hot day than the water from a green coconut.

I found the Tamariis, assisted by an aged Chinaman, preparing *popoi*. They seemed to be at a loss to know how I came to be there, and as neither Louise nor Tumu, her husband, could understand English, they called the old Chinaman to act as interpreter. He said he could speak English, as he had lived in San Francisco some forty years before, but it seemed that he had forgotten most of his Chinese and English and had never learned a great deal of Marquese. After an amusing effort on the part of the Chinaman, I made them understand that I had come from Taiohae with my boat. They then sent a boy to collect eggs, fruit, and coconuts for me to take on board. In the meanwhile my guide had brought out a canoe with which to deliver the provisions along with a party of men and boys who wanted to see the little ship that had come all the way from California. The canoe was launched from the mouth of the stream, and though loaded down till the water was pouring in over the sides, by constant bailing we arrived without having to swim.

Extending along the west side of the bay and of the valley also is an almost perpendicular cliff of fantastically eroded volcanic rock. From off the cliff, more than two thousand feet high, a waterfall plunges down into a dark gorge and at last finds its way through tropical verdure to the sea. The first place that attracted my attention, when I set out to see the valley, was this waterfall, the name of which, Vaipo, I take to mean dark water, or water of night.

On my way through the valley I came across Tumu Tamarii and his man Friday, Chan, busy with their copra. I tried without success to get some information about the waterfall. I might have done better if I had asked about bananas or something to eat, but they did not seem to be able to comprehend any one being interested in a waterfall. A mile or so farther along it came into view. From the road in the valley, a thin ribbon of water was seen streaming down from the heights to disappear in a dark gorge. Leaving the road, I made my way through the jungle that had overgrown numerous pai-pais and stone fences to the entrance of the gorge. For about a quarter of a mile the stream had carved its way back into the rock of the cliff. Fifteen hundred feet in depth, and I could toss a stone from wall to wall! It was an eerie place, and the wild birds that nested among the crags darted down angrily at my head and then soared upward until they were lost to view.

Finding my way back to the road, I followed it into the upper reaches of Hakaui Valley, a beautiful but lonely place. Far up, near where the wild canes take the place of a jungle of trees and vines, I came to a house where two old women beckoned me to stop and sit down. They seemed to know who I was and talked to me all the while in their language, chattering like two children, but not a word did we have in common.

On my way out of the valley I was overtaken by a rainstorm and sought shelter under an overhanging rock, where the *nau-naus* found me out. Tormented by the insects, I fled down the road until I came to a house where a man beckoned with his hand and said come. I sat down in the shelter of his cookhouse, where a smudge was sending up an acrid smoke that to some extent kept the nau-naus at bay, and he opened green coconuts by way of hospitality. We carried on a conversation, so far as a score of words would permit until the shower was over, when he brought out a basket of bananas, and these were added to my load. A short distance above the village the road crossed the stream. I sat down on a boulder and pulled off my shoes, while two small boys, who had a horse tethered on the opposite bank, watched with intense interest. With my camera and tripod slung on my shoulders, my shoes in one hand and the basket of bananas in the other, I waded in. The stones on the bottom were slick and slimy, and out in midstream I slipped and sprawled. In silence, with wide open mouths, the boys stood staring as if they were witnessing a tragedy. I scrambled to my feet laughing and told them that I could swim. They understood not a word, but the spell was broken. They broke into uncontrolled mirth and stood by as I put on my shoes. Dripping wet, I walked on to the village, while they mounted their horse and followed close on my heels, singing and laughing all the way. Once in the village, I knew by the oft repeated word, *Meniki* ("American"), that they were telling to every one we met about what happened to me at the crossing.

This same stream treated me to a new sensation. I was returning to my boat after nightfall and had occasion to take off my shoes for wading it. When I stepped with my bare feet into the water it seemed as if every stone was covered with upturned carpet tacks. By the time I had reached the opposite bank my feet were in a bad way, and I spent an hour or more by the light of the lantern extracting slivers. Investigating the matter, I learned that in the streams of the island there are snails having brittle spines on their shells. They lie concealed among the stones during the day but crawl out on top at night.

My first visit to Hakaui would have been more enjoyable had I understood the language of the inhabitants. Some weeks later I returned to the valley accompanied by Mr. and Mrs. Sterling. As we were going on board, two women with their two children asked to be taken along and thus saved themselves a twelve-mile walk over the rough mountain trail to Hakaui. About halfway to Taioa Bay the wind failed, and we lay rocking about till all the passengers but one of the babies were sick. At last a black cloud that was forming along the shore came driving down on us, and the *Islander* raced away with straining sheets, rain pelting and water streaming off the sails

48

until we were in the entrance. Then like magic we glided out of the storm and into the calm and sunshine of the cove.

Sharing in my enthusiasm for the scenery of the region, the Sterlings went with me to see Ana-o-tako, an old native fort in one of the deep gorges near the Vaipo Falls. Ascending the dry bed of a wash in the bottom of the gorge until we were far above Hakaui Valley, we came to the ruins of a stone wall that had once formed a barrier in the narrow defile. Above the barrier the gorge widened out into a beautiful glen, in which grew many breadfruit trees, some coconuts, and bananas. All about, the walls of the glen rose to a height of a thousand feet or more, and there was no place on the surrounding mountains where an enemy could gain a commanding position over the place. So long as the defenders held the gateway at the narrow entrance they were safe, while a lookout stationed on one of the crags could watch the movements of an enemy in the country around. The young man, who had shown us the way, could tell us little of the history of the place, but he said that in Ana-o-tako the people of Hakaui had once defended themselves when fighting against all the rest of the tribes of Nukahiva.

The next day we went to call on the aged Tahia o Kahe, whom I had met on my former visit. As Mr. Sterling understood her language, we found her interesting. She was the oldest native on Nukahiva, if not in all the Marquesas, and was probably well past the century mark. In all her long life she had been out of Hakaui Valley but twice. She could remember well the birth of her friend Taihina, who was herself very old and almost blind. We asked her of the time when the people of Hakaui had been besieged in Ana-o-tako.

Her eyes brightened and she said, "I was there. It was when Bishop Dordillon was ruling the islands. We were heathens then, while all the rest of the people had become Christians and accepted the priest. For that reason King Moana gathered together all the fighting men of Nukahiva and Uapu and attacked us. We went up into Ana-o-tako. They burned our houses and filled our mar pits full of stones, but they could not get us."

She seemed to get a great deal of satisfaction out of the fact that they were able to beat off their assailants, though later they became reconciled and gave up their old heathen rites. She said she had seen her people die, and now that she was old and useless she wished to join them.

When we were getting under way to return to Taiohae, a canoe loaded with Hakaui people, friends of the Sterlings, put off on the way to the same destination. Going to windward in an overloaded canoe is not comfortable, so the women and children of the party were taken on board the *Islander*.

Getting out of Taioa Bay under sail does not look good. It is obstructed by the cliffs, the wind is baffling, and a strong current sets onto the long rocky point on the west side of the entrance. A heavy swell boiled and foamed over the rocks on either hand as we tacked about the narrow entrance in a light head wind. We would scarce get headway on one tack before it was time to go on the other. I suppose my party, babies and all, could swim, but I had some anxious moments when the *Islander,* her bowsprit close to the rock wall that hemmed us in, would stagger to the top of a swell with scant headway to come about. My companions did not seem to sense the danger, but I felt a great deal easier when we were clear of the cliffs that shut off the trade wind.

Back at Taiohae we found the three-masted schooner, *Tahitian Maiden,* at anchor. I received a call from her skipper, Captain Joe Winchester, and after looking over the *Islander* he invited me on board his ship for dinner. I found him very interesting, as he had come to the islands when a boy, and his great fund of anecdotes were the annals of many years of sailing the South Seas. One American author has made himself famous telling some of Captain Winchester's stories as adventures of his own.

Going on shore I found Dr. and Mrs. Forest Brown. Dr. Brown, a botanist, was making a survey of the Marquesas for the Bishop Museum, and they had come over from Uapu Island in a whaleboat manned by natives. They with Mr. and Mrs. Sterling and myself made quite an American colony in the place.

I spent many interesting days and some busy ones as well, climbing about among the ruined pai-pais and getting photographs of the scenery. Sometimes Mr.

Sterling went with me and sometimes Tapi, but often I went alone. I had another comrade also, a small boy five or six years old, the adopted son of McKittrick's housekeeper. His name was Kai, but they called him Pidgeon's *tumiti* (Pidgeon's son). He followed me about like a dog after its master, raising a great row if any one tried to prevent his going. He chatted incessantly, but he never said a word that I understood, and I am sure he understood none of my talk. However, some strange wisdom came out of his little head, and McKittrick sometimes translated it for me. Once, when his adopted mother was correcting him for some of his headstrong ways, he said to her, "Who is going to feed you, when I go to America with Meniki?"

It was Tapi who pointed out to me a great gray rock that could be seen standing out above the jungle on the slope rising from the west side of the bay. He said it stood on two feet, and as it was one of the wonders of the place, we went to see it. Making our way through the bushes and vines that grew over the pai-pais of a generation that had passed away, we reached the foot of the rock. It stood on the brink of a slight eminence that added to its apparent height, but it rose about seventy feet above its base. The base was a stratum of softer material than the rock above and had weathered away leaving two small supports on which the great mass was balanced, and one wondered why it had not long since toppled over into the ravine below. The rock was called *Putukiaoa* or

Skull Rock, and in former days it had been used as a repository for the skulls of the dead. Among the Marquesans the head was looked upon as a sacred part of the body, and it was an insult to pass anything over the head of another. After death friends sought to place the head of the deceased where it could not be desecrated by any evilly disposed person, so up among the grass and ferns on top of Putukiaoa, the people living in the vicinity placed the heads of those they loved. One of the steps in the march of civilization on Nukahiva was to bring Chinese coolies for laborers, and wherever the Chinese coolie goes he takes leprosy and opium, both of which were introduced among the natives. I was told that a collector once came to Nukahiva and offered to buy some skulls. In order to get the price of the drug, opium users climbed up and took the skulls off Putukiaoa.

From the balanced rock we wandered down to the shore, where, in the shade of a large tamarind tree, stood a house of European design. It was the last house on the shore, deserted and lonely. This had been the house of Queen Vaikehu, and it was here that she received Robert Louis Stevenson when he came to Taiohae. On the opposite side of the road was a large stone platform: the pai-pai where once had stood the house of King Moana. As we looked on the pile of stones, Tapi told me of the time—he was a young man then—when the Kanakas gathered and danced day and night on King Moana's pai-pai, but all was silent now; silent as the near-by tomb where rest the remains of Moana and Vaikehu, the last king and queen of the Marquesas.

The most charming account of the Taiohae people I have read is that of Fanning, who was royally entertained by them when he sailed into the bay with his ship, the *Betsy,* in 1798. About half a mile inland from Queen Vaikehu's house we came to the location where once had been the public meeting ground, or *coeka,* where the chiefs of Taiohae received Fanning. The ruined pai-pais and scattered blocks of stone gave one little idea of what the place had been like, but the noble banyan tree standing at the entrance lifted its head as proudly as it did when it looked down on the gay scene that Fanning tells about in his *Voyages.*

At the far end of the ground lived Nicko, a withered old Kanaka. In broken words Nicko began to tell me of himself, but it was not till he said he came from the island where the *tikis* were that I understood that he was an Easter Island man, and that he was speaking of the great stone images that have been a mystery to visitors of that lonely isle. He spoke of the time, it was in 1862, when Peruvian slavers came to his island and carried away more than three hundred of his countrymen, who died toiling on the guano fields of the Chincha Islands. He himself had been brought to labor on the plantations of Tahiti some fifty years before, but for thirty years he had been living here in the Marquesas.

One day, in order to get a better view of Taiohae Bay, I climbed to the top of the highest peak overlooking the region. When I had almost gained the summit, I came to a deep cut that had been excavated through the mountain ridge from side to side. The marks of the workmen's tools were still to be seen on the gray rock. From the upper side of the cut the top of the peak had been leveled off to a flat floor, and beyond this leveled area there was another cut through the ridge. At first sight one was likely to attribute a work of this kind to some other race than that of the natives, but evidently it was the site of the native fort that Captain Porter mentions in his *Journal.* This he describes as being built on the highest peak overlooking the bay, and protected on either side by a deep cut or fosse that was plainly discernible from his encampment. No other point on the island had so wide an outlook as this peak. Far below was spread out the lovely Bay of Taiohae where the *Islander* lay at anchor, and on the other hand it overlooked the Happar Valley and the Vale of Typee. On my way down I stopped at the house of Repoy, the Happar. Standing on his pai-pai, the cuts could be seen clear against the sky. Pointing to them, I asked him who had made them. "Kanaka made before!" he exclaimed, and went through the motion of firing a gun, to indicate what the place had been used for.

During my voyage I only indulged in one horseback ride, and that was here on Nukahiva. One of my teeth blew up and the resulting pain spread over the whole side of my face. I had seen Mr. Sterling extracting teeth for the natives, but at the time he was at Hatiheu, on the other side of the island. I decided to go over and consult him, and Commissioner Alexander loaned me his horse for the journey. The saddle did not fit me, and the horse was a rough rider. The twenty miles of winding mountain trail were covered somewhat quicker than I would have made it on foot, but I was as tired when I arrived as if I had walked.

Mr. Sterling very effectively removed the cause of my troubles, and then I began to notice what a beautiful place Hatiheu was. The breeze blowing fresh from the sea tempered the heat, and to some extent drove the sand flies away. A clear, cool brook came down from the mountains, and just before it joined the white surf on the shore it formed a pool in the shade of the coconut and breadfruit trees, where I had a refreshing bath.

In the evening as we sat on the veranda of Sterling's house, listening to the low murmuring voices of the natives who had gathered around, I heard an old woman repeat the name, "Tommo." Sterling questioned her, and he said she was talking about an American, who long ago had lived with the Typees. We thought she spoke of Melville. Sterling told her of Melville and of the book he had written. After meditating over it for a time, she said, "This American came to our island in the old days, then he returned to his own country and wrote a book about what he saw, and now the Americans know more about the ways of our fathers than we do ourselves."

The next day when I began the return journey I was rather saddle sore. The horse seemed stiff in his front legs when he was going downhill, and the jar he transmitted to me was something awful. I soon adopted the expedient of riding when going uphill and walking when going downhill. As the day warmed up, he seemed tired, and it took a lot of encouraging to get him to move along. When walking I had a towing job on my hands. I began to feel real sorry for the old fellow, but when we were approaching Taiohae he suddenly broke into a furious gallop, and we brought up in front of the old Government House with a grand flourish.

The water of Taiohae Bay had a constant temperature of about 82°, but after a sweltering day inland a plunge was quite refreshing, and one of the pleasures of my stay at the island was swimming about my boat. There was talk of sharks, and I saw some enormous ones in the waters around the island, but I don't believe they often ventured inside the bay. The sea urchins, of which there were several varieties, troubled me more. There was one with slender spines two or three inches long and sharp as needles. These latter were a great annoyance to the fishermen wading along the shore, for the spines will penetrate even the horny soles of the native's feet. While attempting to land on some rocks I came in contact with one, with the result that my foot resembled a pincushion. The spines are difficult to remove and very painful. My foot became so swollen that I could not wear my shoe, and one of the spines made its way through my toe and came out on the other side several days afterwards.

On several occasions I tried comparing my timepiece with the chronometers of the trading schooners calling at the island, but none of the skippers seemed to have much confidence in their instruments. They never had a rate for them and only carried them to comply with the French marine law. When I asked Captain Alex Doom, of *Tereora,* if he had a chronometer, he said he had, and that there was a card with it showing when it had been last repaired and rated, and that was before he was born.

Captain Alex Doom had grown up in the island trade. His father, a native of Des Moines, Iowa, had gone to Tahiti for his health, and liked the place so well that he settled there and took one of the brown island girls for a wife. He built a small cutter and taught himself navigation. For many years he sailed his craft on trading voyages among the islands, and as his sons grew up he taught them the ways of the sea. It seems that Iowa has produced some seafaring men.

On February 22nd, according to the chronometer of the *Aldebaran,* a French war vessel that was making the round of the islands, my time was sixteen seconds slow. It had been thirty seconds slow when I sailed from Los Angeles.

The largest and fairest valley of Nukahiva is the Vale of Typee, or *Taipi Vai,* as the natives call it. Taipi Vai is the Marquese for high tide, but in this instance, I presume, it refers to the stream flowing through the valley, which is the largest of the island, literally Big Creek. Melville has made the valley famous in his *Typee,* and Captain Porter has given a stirring account of the valor of its inhabitants in his *Journal.* Like most travelers who have visited Nukahiva, I had read *Typee* and came to look over the scene of that wonderful story. The road from Taiohae to Hatiheu runs through the valley, and I had passed that way, but I was not to leave the island until I had paid a visit in the *Islander* to the spacious Comptroller Bay where the vale opens out.

As I sailed from Taiohae Bay, a sudden gust of wind coming down off the mountain caught the mainsail and gybed it over. To ease the shock, I reached for the mainsheet to haul it in, but missing my hold, my arm was caught in a bight of the rope, which straightened out with great violence. A ruptured blood vessel underneath the surface caused my arm to swell to an alarming proportion, and any attempt to use it was painful. It was a very inconvenient time to have my right arm injured; however, I held on my way and later managed to get the anchor down and the sails taken in close by the shore, where Melville escaped from the Typees.

The next morning, after learning that I could use the dinghy without causing too much pain in my injured arm, I set out to see something of the Typee Valley that extends inland from the head of Comptroller Bay. The land on the foreshore was occupied by an experimental farm belonging to a French trading company, where a jovial tattooed native was caring for some pigs. For lack of a common language our conversation was limited, but he made me understand that he was a native of Houmi Valley, and intimated that the Typees had been man-eaters. He pointed out a peak on the ridge between Typee and Houmi Valley where he said the people of Houmi had once had a fort from which they could watch the Typees. That I might have a better view of Typee, I climbed up onto the ridge. Down below where the white surf broke on the beach, Captain Porter landed his force from the *Essex* to make his first attack on the warring Typees, and from the same beach Melville had escaped in Karakoee's whaleboat. To-day no savage war cries sounded from the shore, and only the gentle murmur of the surf reached the ear, but beautiful still in silence lay mountain and vale. Rank after rank of hibiscus, mapu, and banyan trees waved over the pai-pais of the dead warriors, while above and beyond the forest wild canes, vines, and ferns clung even to the topmost crags.

The pretty Houmi Valley on the other side of the ridge tempted me and I wandered down into the shade of its trees. Near the sea a brook ran through a quiet reach that was beautiful as fairyland, and merry children swam in the clear water. On the green bank of the stream was a small village where the people made me welcome. But I found no one that I could converse with, so after refreshing myself with bananas

THE VALE OF TYPEE, THE SCENE OF HERMAN MELVILLE'S
"TYPEE."

VAIAHU FALLS, IN THE VALE OF TYPEE, WHERE MELVILLE AND
TOBY DESCENDED INTO THE VALLEY.

"AHUA," THE TABU PAI PAI WHERE THE TYPEES KEPT THE
SKULLS OF THEIR ENEMIES.

HAKATAU AND POI UTU, THE LAST OF THE TYPEES.

and a drink from a green coconut I returned to the Typee side.

Taking my dinghy into the Taipi Vai I rowed upstream for about half a mile to where overhanging trees barred farther progress with a boat. Near the head of navigation I came to a house where a man, whose legs were paralyzed, sat carving rosewood bowls. He must have been lonely, for he beckoned me to come near. With some difficulty we managed to exchange a few ideas. I learned that he was a native of Houmi Valley, and he introduced his wife as an American, saying that her father, Henry Nichols, had come from New York, but she appeared to know less of the American language than her husband.

During the last war between the United States and Great Britain, Captain Porter, of the U. S. S. *Essex,* then cruising in the Pacific, having captured several British whalers, came to Taiohae Bay in order to make some necessary repairs. He made a treaty with the chiefs of Taiohae, and even went so far as to take possession of the island in the name of the United States. But some of the tribes of Nukahiva, notably the Typees, were not so friendly to the Americans as the Taiohaes, and the presence of Porter's force in their midst soon brought on hostilities. Porter of a necessity took up the cause of his allies. He first settled a little difficulty with the Happars, and then turned his attention to the Typees, who were the irreconcilable enemies of both the Happars and the

Taiohaes. Peaceful negotiations having failed, he made a demonstration with force.

He landed a small force on the beach at the head of Comptroller Bay and attacked the Typees. After penetrating for about half a mile into the valley the Americans came to a stone fortification, where the Typees made a stand. With his force reduced to less than twenty men, and receiving no support from his native allies, Porter was forced to retreat to his boats. Knowing that defeat would end in his being driven off the island, Porter returned to Taiohae, and after mustering a force of some two hundred and fifty men, marched overland on a second expedition. Crossing over the mountains, they came down into the hostile valley not far from the fortification where the first conflict took place. Confronted by this larger force and an army of Taiohae and Happar warriors, the Typees made an obstinate resistance, fighting with spears and throwing stones from slings. However, the Typees, defeated and their homes laid waste, sued for peace and paid an indemnity of four hundred pigs. To this day Captain Porter is remembered with respect by the people of Nukahiva.

There is still standing in the valley a stone wall that is pointed out as the scene of the battle between Captain Porter's force and the Typees. It is called Porter's Pai-pai. Having heard of it before I came to the valley, I questioned the bowl maker as to its location. It took a lot of talk to get him to understand, but he seemed to know of it. A tall native, who was standing by at the time, said, "I will show you." He was Poi Utu, a Typee. He had a limited knowledge of English and, becoming my guide, told me what he could of the native history and tradition.

Porter's Pai-pai is a rude stone wall standing on the hillside about two hundred yards back from the stream and running parallel with it for a like distance. The wall was about five or six feet thick at the base and half that at the top and of a suitable height for a man standing behind it to throw a stone over. In the immediate vicinity Poi pointed out locations where other parts of the defensive works had stood at the time of Porter's invasion. Taking into consideration its distance from the shore of the bay and its location near where the road crosses the stream, it is probable that this was the place where the Typees turned back Porter's force on their first attempt to invade the valley. As we walked through the silent and almost deserted vale Poi told me the native tradition of the fight with Porter.

When Captain Porter invaded the valley for the second time, the Typees sent their women and children over the mountain to Atiheu, where the people were their allies, and as Porter's force advanced through the valley the warriors retreated in the same direction. At a small stream that he pointed out, Poi said Porter had turned back from pursuing the Typees, and down in the valley we came to the ruins of a large public feasting ground where he said the Americans had stopped to rest when returning from the fight.

As we wandered among the deserted pai-pais, Poi could recall the name of the family whose home every prominent one had been. While examining one of these that was about thirty feet square and eight feet high, I discovered an opening on the top leading down into it and off to one side. Poi said this was a place where the dwellers on the pai-pai could conceal their property in case of war and they had to retreat, as they did when Porter invaded their valley. The opening had been in that part of the house where it would have been covered with the sleeping mats, and no doubt there had once been a stone fitted to close and conceal it.

Occasionally as we passed along, Poi would point to some location and say, "Tabu pai-pai, Kanaka no go there," and he would pass by another way. He was referring to some spot on which, because of some event that had taken place there, a tabu had been placed that was to forever make it sacred from the intrusion of men.

One day, when out alone, I came across one of these tabu places. At the foot of an ancient banyan tree was a pai-pai about fifteen feet square and four feet high. In it was a pit about three feet across. How deep the pit was I could not see, for it was full of skulls. This, then, was the place where the Typees had kept the skulls of such of their enemies as had been unfortunate enough to fall into their hands.

A small house had once occupied one-half of the pai-pai, arranged so that the pit would be right in front of it, and in this house had lived a warrior priest, who guarded the skulls and kept them under his feet in a ceremonial way. When one of these priests died his body was put in the trunk of the banyan tree in such a manner that the ever-growing roots thrown down from above would grow over and incase it. Thus, even in death the priest still kept guard.

This particular tree was decaying on the inside, and the skeletons of the warrior priests were falling to the ground. Finding an opening between the ropelike roots, I passed into the hollow interior of the ancient tree. My attention was attracted to a large skull lying partly covered with fragments of rotten wood. At some time, probably early in life, this man had been struck a terrible blow over the right eye. Whatever weapon he had been struck with had crushed its way through the bony arch over the eye, and a deep bone scar below the eye socket showed where its course had been arrested. The eye must have been destroyed. Another blow had knocked out the four upper incisors. As I gazed on the skull, the thought flashed through my mind that this was the head of Melville's friend, the one-eyed Chief Mow-Mow. No other could have been better qualified to act as guardian of the grim trophies.

When I described the place to Poi, he said, "Tabu pai-pai," but I learned something of its history. The name of the place was Ahau. In the days when the tribes were waging a feudal warfare with one another, each tribe had a similar place in which to keep their trophies. I had examined a similar pai-pai at Taiohae, from which the skulls had been removed.

I asked Poi about Melville, and he went with me to the pai-pai where once had stood the house of Tokuhi, a chief under whose protection two Americans had lived in the old days. He had made them tabu so they were safe to go and come about the valley where they would. They had lived for a time in Typee and then went away to Taiohae, but their names Poi did not know. In the upper reaches of the valley, near where the road begins to wind its way over the mountain to Atiheu, we came to an ancient feasting ground. It had been just such a place as Melville describes as the "hoola hoola" ground, and what the Marquesans call a *coeka*. This coeka, to which Poi gave the name of Hanaei, was located on a narrow strip of ground between the present road and a mountain stream that ran below. A retaining wall near twenty feet high had been built up from the bed of the stream and the space above filled in to make a level area on which had been the tabu ground, or holy place, where, according to Poi, no woman was allowed to enter. Here was one of the most extensive collections of pai-pais in the valley, and so thickly overgrown with trees that I had not noticed it though I had passed that way several times before. At the far end of the terrace there was a pai-pai about seventy-five feet in length and a third that in width and three feet high, where once had stood the house of Chief Tokuhi, the friend of the two Americans. It is not at all improbable that Tokuhi

66

was the Mehevi of Melville, and that this was the place where he saw the bodies of the slain Happars carried for the feast.

On the hillside near the tabu ground was a pit that had been excavated in the rock about thirty feet deep and fourteen feet square. Here, Poi said, had been stored the surplus breadfruit during years of plenty. He said there had been six coekas in the valley, belonging to as many different clans, and each clan had one of these great storage pits as well. Poi had a tradition of a time when for seven years there was not enough rain to cause the breadfruit to bear and most of the breadfruit and coconut trees died.

The breadfruit, when peeled and fermented, runs together in a doughy mass. This when packed in pits and covered with a thick layer of *ti* leaves and then earth to exclude the air will keep in an edible condition for years. Popoi, a preparation of fermented breadfruit, is the staple food of the natives of the Marquesas.

Everywhere through the valley were evidences of a once dense population. Captain Porter counted twenty-six hundred fighting men in the Typee valley. Melville estimated the population of the valley as several thousand. At the time of Poi's earliest recollection they had been reduced to about three hundred individuals. At the time of my visit there were about twenty-five inhabitants in the valley, and only two were pure Typees, the rest being half-castes or natives of some other locality who had settled there.

Once when speaking of the destruction of his race after the coming of the white man, Poi, his eyes blazing with indignation, pointed to his foot swollen with elephantiasis and said, "Kanaka was never sick before." Elephantiasis was introduced when the French brought prisoners suffering with that disease from the Society Islands to the Marquesas. The French, he said, had once passed a law forbidding them to eat popoi, saying it was eating rotten breadfruit that made them die so fast. "We told them," said he, "you have made many laws and we have tried to obey them, but we have always eaten popoi and were never sick before you came. Put us all in prison, for we are going to eat popoi anyhow."

There has been some speculation as to the reason for the inordinate appetite of the Polynesians for fermented food. In my opinion, it fills some real need in their diet. Most Europeans use fermentation in the preparation of their bread. Dieticians, it seems, have discovered a lack of some properties they call vitamines in our food, and many people have taken to eating yeast to supply the need. It is possible the Kanaka long ago realized the deficiency in vitamines of his food supply, and anticipated his more civilized brethren in taking up the yeast eating habit.

When I went to call on Poi for the last time, he gave me the largest bunch of bananas I had ever seen. I wanted to help carry it to my boat, but that was not the way of the Typees. I must not be seen carrying it. Having suspended the bananas on a pole, Poi

A HOME IN THE MARQUESAS.

MARQUESANS PREPARING "POPOI" FROM BREADFRUIT.

PEARL DIVERS OF TAKAROA ISLAND, WAITING THEIR TURNS AT THE BARBER SHOP.

TAKAROA MAIDENS MAKE THEIR OWN HATS.

shouldered the heavy end while Jeanne D'arc, his adopted daughter, took up the other, and laden with their gift, they accompanied me to the shore.

In tropical waters the underwater part of a vessel fouls rapidly, and during the time she had been anchored in the harbors of Nukahiva the *Islander* had accumulated a considerable marine growth. Anaho Bay, on the north side of the island, was recommended as the best place to beach a boat for repairs, and there I took advantage of the spring tide to clean and paint the bottom of the *Islander*. After two weeks in Typee I sailed around the east end of Nukahiva and dropped the anchor in Anaho Bay.

Anaho Bay was Robert Louis Stevenson's first port of call when he sailed to the South Seas in the *Casco*. Anaho Bay is still a beautiful place, though Stevenson's friends are there no more. Only one or two families reside there now. Several people came from Atiheu Bay to see me, but none that I could converse with. They had the kindliest smiles though and came to see the *Islander* bringing presents of such fruits as they had. A troop of Atiheu children came over and had great sport with my dinghy, then ran off into the jungle and came back with a hatful of eggs from the nests of wild chickens that abounded there. One bright little boy of Anaho took a great fancy to my dinghy and went away to come back with a man, presumably his father, who examined it carefully. I could see that my little friend was pleading to have one like it made for himself. After nightfall the reef on the shore of the bay was lit up with the torches of the natives, who came there to spear fish.

But all the while I was at work on the *Islander*. Cleaning and painting the bottom of a boat is hard work under any circumstances and this time it was a painful task. The nau-naus had developed an abscess on one of my arms and the other was still sore and swollen from the accident I had met with when sailing from Taiohae Bay. I ran the *Islander* on the beach at high tide and as the water fell went at the bottom with scraper and brush. For three days I had scarce time to sleep. Day and night I had to watch for each turn of the tide, and when one side was finished, warp the boat around and down so that I could work on the other side. It was night when I had finished and kedged the *Islander* off into deep water, but I was too tired and sore to sleep well.

I sailed from Anaho Bay at sunrise. As soon as I was out of the bay, the trade wind blowing strong out of the east sent the *Islander* flying away on one of the most wonderful sails I have ever had. I sailed to the west by Atiheu, Hakapu, and Vakao Bay, by dark cliffs and headlands and on into the calm under the lee of the island. Then I met the wind coming down the south side of the island and beat up against it to Taiohae, after having sailed around the most romantic island I have ever visted.

A few busy days at Taiohae and then I was ready to put to sea once more. The Tuamotu Islands, lying between the Marquesas and Tahiti, have rather a bad reputation on account of the number of vessels that have been wrecked there, and some advised me to avoid them altogether, but I was very anxious to see something of the atolls. I had no charts of the group other than a track chart of the whole Pacific Ocean, but with the help of the sailing directions and information I had obtained from the skippers of the trading schooners, who are continually plying between the Society, Tuamotu, and Marquesas Islands, I decided to call at Takaroa. The Tuamotu Islands have a great sameness of appearance, but Takaroa, standing well out on the north side of the group, is easy to approach and once sighted would be readily identified on account of a wreck of a large ship that was still standing on the reef.

V

The Passage through the Tuamotus to Tahiti and the Society Islands

AT noon on May 3, 1922, I sailed from Nukahiva, carrying the blessings of its kind inhabitants. My ship was laden with its fruits. The wind was light, but at dusk Uapu, the island of night, lay abeam. When morning came no land was in sight. The wind continued light, and I drifted slowly to south by west, at times reminded of the doldrums.

On the third day out, in a calm, I plunged over the side and swam around the boat. I started on another round, but, seized with some sudden apprehension, I turned back and climbed quickly on board to look over the stern just as a shark came swimming up. The shark was accompanied by a striped fish that always swam just over his back, while several small fish had attached themselves to his sides and were traveling at his expense. He kept continually swimming alongside and underneath the boat, rubbing against the hull as if trying to rid himself of his passengers. He followed the boat all day, and only left off after I had wounded him twice with the boat hook.

One night I went below to sleep, leaving the boat sailing with all sails set. About midnight I was awakened by a roar of wind and rain. The wind was driving the rain in a horizontal flood, while the *Islander* was tearing along, leaning over till the boom trailed in the sea and leaving a wake of phosphorescent foam behind. Springing to the main halyards I let the sail come down, and brought the yawl into the wind under jib and mizzen sails. In about half an hour the squall had passed, leaving a fresh southeast breeze blowing. An occasional squall freshened the wind, and the *Islander* glided on until my calculation indicated that I was close up to the islands.

On the morning of May 12th, I came early on deck and made sail after having drifted with the jib during the night. When daylight broke over the sea, a feathery line appeared on the horizon. It was Takaroa Island and my first sight of a coral atoll. Coasting along off the shore, I passed the great four-masted ship, *County of Roxburg,* high on the jagged reef. There was little wind blowing when I came up off the pass into the lagoon, but the tide was running in like a river, and I had no difficulty in entering. The village is just inside the entrance, and Elder Burbidge, the local Mormon missionary, came off in a canoe to assist in bringing the *Islander* alongside the wharf, where I distributed the remains of the bananas and other fruit among a crowd of smiling islanders, who had gathered to greet me.

There is something entrancing about the scenery when one sails for the first time into the lagoon of a coral atoll. Just a wreath of verdure cast upon the

73

sea, a thin fringe of coconut trees and bushes enclosing the calm waters of the lagoon, but down below all this was an enchanted underwater world where wonderful fishes dart or glide in and out of the coral caves, all colors and shapes, from monsters to butterflies. And on the inner reef, where the water is shallow, beautiful shellfish make their home. I never tired of searching for the pretty shells that washed ashore.

The pass into the lagoon is about one hundred and fifty yards wide and a mile long. The water is clear as crystal, and when I sailed in I could see the smallest objects on the green and white bottom, though the depth was eight fathoms. From that depth on either side rises a coral wall full of holes and caverns. It is interesting to watch the boys of the village fishing. They dive down and search the holes in the coral walls of the pass for such fish as are good for food and spear them. In this way they accustom themselves to staying under the water for two or three minutes and prepare for going into the deeper waters of the lagoon after the pearl oysters.

The Takaroa lagoon is about fifteen miles long and five miles wide, fenced in by a narrow coral reef on which grows a thin fringe of coconut trees and a tangle of coarse bushes. Little else will grow on Takaroa without artificial aid, as the hurricanes that occasionally sweep over the Tuamotus wash the soil off, leaving only coarse coral sand and gravel. I was told that the highest land on Takaroa was only six feet above the sea level. A hurricane had swept Takaroa some years before—the same that had landed the *County of Roxburg* on the island—and one man related to me how he had climbed a coconut tree, and the tree had bent under the force of the wind until he was washed by the great seas that swept over the whole island.

Aside from the coconuts and fish most of the food consumed in the island is imported, but I saw a considerable number of dogs about the village, and as there were no wild pigs to hunt, I asked a native of what use they were. He replied, "We eat 'em." I heard a native discussing the relative merits of food, and his opinion, as translated by Elder Burbidge, was "Fish is number one, dog is number two, and beef is number three." However, from proceeds of the pearl fisheries and the sale of dried coconuts, the people seemed quite prosperous. The women were skillful hat-makers, and the girls appeared in church with the most wonderful millinery, no two hats being alike. I was told that they had more than twenty-five patterns of braid from which to make hats.

The people of the island are for the most part Mormons, having been converted by missionaries of that denomination from America. I was exchanging ideas with the men of the village, and they asked me what sect I belonged to. I told them that I was a Quaker. This was a mystery to them, as their knowledge of the subject was limited to Roman Catholics and Mormons, but after discussing the question among themselves, they decided that a Quaker and a Mormon were about the same thing.

All able-bodied Tuamotuans are divers and most of them are sailors as well. They took great interest in my voyage and my craft and had the name *Islander* painted on the beacon at the end of the wharf by the side of *Speejacks,* the name of an American yacht that had called there some time before.

I sailed from Takaroa Island for Tahiti at noon on May 17th. Makitua, the village policeman, helped me to make sail and get under way, and then when we were outside the pass, he swam to the reef and walked back.

A change in the weather had set in while I was resting at Takaroa; the wind was blowing strong, while occasionally one of the squalls, for which the Tuamotus are famous, came driving along. Takaroa was soon lost to view. I went flying by Takapoto from which I lay a course to bring me in sight of Apataka. The day ended with stormy weather, and I took in the mainsail. A little later the mizzen halyard parted, letting that sail come down, and I let the *Islander* run under the jib for the night. As soon as there was a little light, I put up the mainsail and began scanning the horizon for coconut trees. Soon after daybreak I sighted Apataka, its low feathery outline dim through the rain. Two hours later I sighted Kaukura. The wind increased, and I reefed the mainsail. A squall swept down, driving right onto the island, but by noon I had weathered the great reef at the southeast end of Kaukura, and lay a course for Tahiti, clear of the

Tuamotus, on whose reefs the timbers of many a stout vessel have bleached.

After clearing the Tuamotus, the wind fell light, though the sea and sky had a threatening look. The next afternoon the wind came out of the south with a fierce squall, but the terrifying aspect of the sky and the angry sea rolling on ahead of the gale gave warning of what was coming, and the *Islander* met it under short sail. Awed as I was at the sight of the approaching storm, I felt a thrill of joy as she rode off before it. With the coming of darkness I hove to as I did not wish to come up with the Island of Tahiti on a stormy night.

When I came on deck at daybreak, the wind had died out to a good sailing breeze. I had not been able to get a satisfactory sight of the sun the day before, but Maitea Island, standing out high and blue on the southern horizon, set at rest any doubts I had as to my position. Before noon a dark bank of clouds rolled away and right ahead Tahiti lay in the sunlight. But the wind was falling light, and it was midnight when I came up off Point Venus light, where I lay to until morning, enjoying the fragrance of the offshore breeze that blew gently out from this matchless isle.

No other isle of the southern seas has a more gorgeous appearance than Tahiti. When the sun rose over this scene of island splendor, I was gliding along outside the barrier reef looking for the entrance to Papeete Harbor, and called to mind the words of Charles Warren Stoddart, when sea-weary and land-hungry, he wrote of his approach to Tahiti in *South Sea Idyls*.

I arrived at Papeete on May 21st. My coming had been heralded by the crews of trading schooners I had met in Taiohae, and a crowd, including several Americans and other English-speaking residents, gathered to welcome me to the isle. After I had given an account of myself to the inquiring throng, I set about seeing something of my new surroundings. Interested residents, who came to see the *Islander* and to hear about the voyage, volunteered to show me around and took me on excursions about the country.

One does not see much of Papeete when approaching from the sea, for it is hidden away under immense shade trees that make it a quiet, restful place. I found myself quite happy there.

Tahiti is a beautiful isle, well watered, and wrapped about and caressed by the balmy air of a climate that is almost perfect. The island is a lofty and precipitous mountain, with a narrow strip of lowland around its base. There is heavy rainfall on the mountains, and numerous rivers and rivulets radiate in all directions from the central highlands and find their way in many a cascade and fall to the sea. When traveling about the island, one is never far from one of these beautiful streams. Every one lives on the narrow strip of coast land. If you take the road that winds along the shore and follow it around the island, you will meet almost the entire population, and a more beautiful drive than this highway between mountain and sea, you will find

THE ISLANDER AT TAKAROA.

BATHING COSTUME, PAPEETE, TAHITI.

THE ISLANDER AT THE ESPLANADE, PAPEETE, TAHITI, WITH
MUREA IN THE DISTANCE.

THE ISLANDER ANCHORED IN PAOPAO BAY, MUREA ISLAND.

nowhere. But even in this island Eden, modern inventions are found to make land travel dangerous.

A few days after my arrival, a party of Americans called to take me for a drive along the coast to Taravao. On the way back to Papeete, one of the party, who was driving, tried to show how they do it in California, and while we were rounding a sandy curve in the road at an accelerated speed, a wheel collapsed, and the ancient flivver rolled over. No one was hurt, but I remembered that my friends had often said I was not born to be drowned.

There is rain on the mountains almost every day, and the jungle is all but impenetrable, so mountain climbing is not popular here, though it would have been interesting to have followed one of the native men, who go up there to bring down the *feis* that grow in the highlands.

But easier to see than the mountains, and wonderfully interesting, are the coral reefs that form a barrier almost entirely around the Island of Tahiti. For the variety and beauty of their corals, fishes, and shell, they are second only to the reefs of the Tuamotus. There is a peculiarity in the tides throughout the Society Islands that I noticed first in Papeete Harbor. High tide always occurs at about midday and again at midnight.

There are many places of interest to see in Tahiti, if one has the energy to find them, but on the whole, it is easier to go to the morning market, or sit in the shade and hear tales of strange adventure, told by men from the ends of the earth. On the esplanade near where the *Islander* lay were some magnificent trees, in the shade of which gathered the men of leisure to discuss the questions of the day. Here, and at the Sunday morning market, one could meet all the characters of Papeete who were worth knowing. There was no newspaper published in Papeete, but the Sunday morning market answered every purpose. The men talked, the girls bought garlands of flowers with which to deck themselves, and the housewives laid in a supply of fruits, fish, and vegetables.

On May 31st, the American yacht *Invader,* of Santa Barbara, came in and lay alongside of the *Islander.* The owner, Mr. J. P. Jefferson, who was interested in island history, was making an extensive cruise through the islands of the Pacific and came to Tahiti from Marquesas. For a time this beautiful yacht quite eclipsed the little yawl lying alongside, but the party on board was not getting any more enjoyment out of their cruise than was the crew of the *Islander.*

One morning I was sitting on my boat watching the tourists coming ashore from the S. S. *Maruru* that had just arrived from San Francisco, when a man hove alongside and said, "You don't know who I am."

"Oh, yes, I do, your name is Thompson," I said.

Thompson was a man who had wanted to join me when I was preparing to sail from Los Angeles. He had been on a voyage to the South Seas when he was a young man, and at seventy-two years of age wanted to return with me on the *Islander.* He tried to interest me in a trading venture, but I was not interested in trading, and, besides, was going alone. But here he was a year later, a passenger on the *Maruru* bound for New Guinea, he said, where he intended ending his days. The island life grows on one.

The fei is a variety of plantain or banana, that takes the same important part in the diet of the Tahitian that breadfruit does with the Marquesan. There is an old South Sea proverb—"If you once eat of the feis of the island, you are under a spell and will have to return to the island." When I dined with my Tahitian friends, they would tell me to eat plenty of feis.

The most important holiday, and the one great event of the year in Papeete is the anniversary of the fall of the Bastille. My friends would say, "You must stay for the Fourteenth of July," or, "You can't go away until after the Fourteenth." What the "Glorious Fourth" is to Americans, the "Fourteenth" was to these French subjects. I had intended leaving before that time, but there was much to do and habits of procrastination flourish in this mellow atmosphere, so I helped to celebrate *"Jour de Bastille"* in Papeete.

Many an evening I watched the sun set behind the fantastic peaks of Murea Island, leaving them a silhouette against the gorgeous red and gold of the sky; then one day I sailed across the channel to Murea and anchored in beautiful Paopao Bay.

On the shore of the bay lived a Raiatean, who had come there to look for buried treasure. He sought me out and invited me to come to his house to eat and to talk. He spoke English and said he would lose the language if he had no one to talk it with. He had a map of the bay that was supposed to indicate the location where a fabulous sum of Spanish-American gold was buried. It was very romantic to find a South Sea islander digging for pirates' treasure, but I think he was getting discouraged about finding the gold, for he had rented a piece of land and had made a good start for a plantation.

With a native boy for a guide, I walked across country to Popetoai Bay. There was no road, but for a time we followed a track made by wild pigs through the forest and then wandered, hot and thirsty, through the wild canes. At last we came down to where herds of cattle were grazing on a beautiful green meadow. We found sweet oranges to quench our thirst and rested in the shade of the trees. It was one of the prettiest spots in the world, and as I looked over the green valley nestling between the mountains, I thought I should like to settle there, and quit the tossing sea; but in the end I wandered back to where the *Islander* lay and made ready to sail.

The wind was light when I sailed from Murea for the Island of Bora Bora, in the leeward group of the Society Islands. At daybreak the next morning I sighted Huaheine Island, while Murea was still in sight astern. A heavy swell was coming up from the southwest against the wind, indicating that a gale was raging in the region of westerly winds. As I came up alongside of Huaheine, the great white rollers rushed in and broke on the reef with a tremendous roar, while the offshore wind was damp and cool with spray. The *Islander* glided leisurely through the channel between Huaheine and Raiatea Island. It was after sunset when I rounded Tahaa Island, and sighted the tower-like peak of Bora Bora. Rain squalls swept down blotting everything from view, and I hove to. The weather cleared with the dawn, and I headed in for the lone peak again.

Bora Bora is a beautiful little island with one high central peak, and the surrounding barrier reef has, for the most part, a fringe of coconut trees, giving the whole the appearance of a volcanic island standing in the lagoon of an atoll. I do not think its like is to be found in all the South Seas.

When I came up to the island I found wind and tide both favorable and sailed into the lagoon, coming to anchor in eight fathoms close to the village.

The only white man on the island was the French gendarme, and he did not speak English. I only met three persons with whom I could carry on a conversation. One of these, Harry Deane, said his father was an American. In the evening Mr. Deane invited me to attend the services, which he called a *himine,* at the native church.

The church, or himine house, was a large, well-ventilated structure, with walls made after the manner of a picket fence, and beautifully thatched with pandanus leaves. A few benches were provided for seats, but most of the congregation sat on the floor, and some stretched out and slept in a comfortable way that would have aroused envy in many a one in a more highly civilized community. A number of the older people made short talks, and between the discourses there was singing. The women did the singing, while the men accompanied them with a peculiar sound given out in an attempt to imitate some musical instrument. My friend explained this by saying that they had no organ. He was the chief musician.

The next morning after my arrival I started out for a walk and asked a young man, Tauraa Ottori, some questions about the island road. He did not seem to understand, but he took it upon himself to accompany me, or rather he exhibited me to the inhabitants of the outlying districts. We called at most every house that we passed, and to every one that we met on the road he seemed to be giving a glowing account of myself, though I understood none of it. I must have met most of the inhabitants of Bora Bora that day. But it was a wonderful jaunt, and we passed right around the central mountain of the island.

The people were busy gathering and drying their coconuts. Some were preparing tapioca from manioc roots. Others were looking after vanilla, a considerable quantity of which is produced on the island. One is continually hearing about how indolent the Kanakas are, but I wondered why they were as industrious as they are.

At Bora Bora I put things in order for the voyage to Samoa, repaired sails and rigging and restowed my supplies, not forgetting to take on a good supply of coconuts and bananas. I went out to look for a source of water supply, thinking to take on a little more, but found no satisfactory place to get it. I tried to inquire, with the result that a boy climbed a tree and brought down some drinking nuts for me.

VI

Samoa

A FEW days at Bora Bora, and then on the morning of August 3rd, I put to sea once more. The wind was light, but when the sun was low, the peak of Bora Bora was but a small blue dot on the eastern horizon. By morning I was clear of Belinghausen Atoll, the last of the coral reefs in the track of the *Islander,* on her way to Samoa.

I was now running before the wind, sailing on night and day, with little to do except to calculate my position and set down the progress of the *Islander* on the chart. Each day the sun came up astern, and as it passed overhead it verified my course across the waters, and then went down in the gorgeous cloudland that always lay ahead.

On August 12th, the wind and sea came rolling up from the south, driven by some commotion in the southern ocean. At sunset the wind and sea were rising, but I held on under short sail and began watching for Manua Island, in the Samoan Group. I sighted Manua at 2:30 o'clock in the morning and came up to the island at sunrise. I ran to the north and under the lee of the land. At Faleasau Bay, on the northwest side of the island, a steamer lay at anchor, and I

POPETOAI BAY, MUREA ISLAND.

BORABORA, THE TYPICAL SOUTH SEA ISLAND.

SAMOAN HOUSES, TUTUILA ISLAND, AMERICAN SAMOA.

THE AMERICAN NAVAL STATION, PANGO PANGO, AMERICAN SAMOA.

thought of taking shelter, but instead put in another reef and sailed on.

All afternoon I sat at the tiller, running off before the worst of the breaking seas, and hoping to close up with Tutuila Island before darkness set in, for I did not know if I would dare try to run into the strange harbor on a stormy night with the wind blowing right on shore.

The sun had set when I came up to the east end of the island. I hastily consulted the chart and sailing directions, and was able to locate the headlands on either side of Pango Pango Harbor. A rain squall was adding to the darkness, but I soon made out the harbor lights. Driving before the squall, I sailed in, let the anchor go, and no one on shore knew that I was there until morning.

When morning came I looked out on mountains on every hand. The harbor turns off at a right angle from the entrance, and from the anchorage the sea is not in sight. From all appearance I might have been in a mountain lake. Strange brown men, bareheaded and wearing loin cloths, went gliding by in outrigger canoes. Occupying a conspicuous position just inside of the turn in the bay, were the white buildings and well-kept grounds of the American Naval Station. Along the shore on either hand were the more picturesque houses of the natives. But above all I was impressed with the fresh and green appearance of the landscape.

While the *Islander* lay at anchor in the shadow of

the mountains, I went on excursions about the green islands. One of the compensations for enduring the solitude of sea was the delight of exploring a new land when I came to it, and here was a land that was my ideal of what a tropical island should be.

American Samoa has an abundance of rain, and from the beach to the mountain tops it was always fresh and green. I am under the impression that it rained every day that I was there. I once asked an old resident if it rained every day in Samoa. He said that he had lived there for twenty years, and had no recollection of a day when it did not rain sometime during the twenty-four hours. However, the rain came in heavy showers, with much bright sunshine in between, and often the sun would shine all day with a downpour in the evening or at night.

Pango Pango has an annual rainfall of about two hundred inches. A mountain at the east side of the bay, called the "Rainmaker," stirred up the trade winds and formed clouds that precipitated their moisture over the bay region. When one of these tropical showers was approaching, one could hear the pattering of the raindrops on the palm leaves across the bay, a mile or so away.

The natives of Tutuila Island still retain many of their primitive customs, and I found no people more interesting.

American Samoa is the only place that I visited in the South Seas where the native population was increasing. One of the first things that I noticed was

88

the number of children playing around their villages. The people have come less in contact with Europeans, and their houses, clothing, and habits of life have changed less than in most of the islands. There is no opportunity there for the acquiring of land for plantations, and the subsequent importation of diseased Asiatics for laborers. Since the establishment of the United States Naval Station, quarantine regulations have been strict, and there have been few epidemics.

When one enters a Samoan village the houses attract the attention at once. They look like nothing else so much as great overgrown mushrooms. Nothing better could be designed for the climate than the Samoan house, which consists of a large umbrella-like roof, supported on posts, and no walls. Mat curtains are arranged around the sides to let down in case of a storm. For a floor, the earth is raised a little above the surrounding surface and covered with coral gravel. The heavily thatched roof is a good protection from rain and sun, and the house is clean, cool, and airy.

During my stay at the island I was often entertained by hospitable natives, and they came to see and to admire the *Islander*. They were interested in my adventures and in the pictures and articles that I had brought from other lands. Often the boys and girls from the near-by villages would swim out and board the *Islander* until there was no more standing room, and never before or since has the *Islander* been boarded by such merry, riotous youngsters.

When I entered a Samoan's house as a guest, one of

the maidens of the household would spread out a mat for me to sit on, and then, instead of tea, she would serve *kava*.

Kava is the national drink of Samoa, and is drunk on all occasions and served with great ceremony. What peculiar properties this emulsion of powdered kava root and water had, I do not know, but many Europeans acquire a taste for it. In former days, the dry kava root was chewed by the younger girls before being mixed with water, but now, under the influence of the more fastidious whites, it is pulverized in a mortar. However, some of the white men, who had lived long in the islands, said the kava was better when made in the old way.

I never saw a Samoan woman or girl drinking kava. Once, when kava was being served, I asked why the girls did not partake. The only explanation they would give was, "Kava is good for boys, not good for girls."

I did not notice the indolence among the natives that is so often spoken of by Europeans. True they may not take to the monotonous toil of civilization, but when living their own normal life, and the occasion calls for it, the islanders expend their energy as freely as any one. The well-developed physique of the unspoiled islander indicates that he takes his exercise.

In their villages I often came upon them busy at some interesting bit of native work that would be displayed for sale on steamer day. Many of their articles, such as tapa cloth, kava bowls, and tortoise shell ornaments, have artistic merit.

SAMOAN CEREMONY OF THE MATS.

Here the social standing of the first families of American Samoa is being determined.

A SAMOAN ARTIST PAINTING TAPA.

A SAMOAN MAIDEN OF TUTUILA ISLAND.

ON TUTUILA ISLAND A MAN CUTS NO FIGURE
IN SOCIETY UNLESS HIS PANTS ARE TATTOOED ON.

The naval band stationed at Pango Pango is composed of native Samoans under the instruction of an American bandmaster. Some of the natives are accomplished musicians. I do not call to mind having enjoyed any music more than I did the notes of the evening band concerts, borne on the soft night air to where the *Islander* lay at anchor in the shadow of the mountains.

I found a kindred spirit in Bandmaster Teubner who went with me on many a jaunt about the island. Mr. Teubner was interested in the songs and music of Samoa, and with the assistance of his bandmen was setting them down in writing.

One of our hikes was to Vaitongi, the scene of a Samoan legend about a boy and a girl who sacrificed themselves by leaping off a rock into the sea. According to the legend they were changed into a turtle and a shark. There is a song about them, and now it is said that when the boys and girls of the village stand on the rock and sing the song, a turtle and a shark appear in the sea below.

We had rather a hazy idea of the distance, and took Vaimili, the drummer, along for a guide. Vaimili was not enthusiastic about walking to the place, said it was too far. We started in the early morning, and by noon we had found out that the guide was right when he said it was too far. But we passed through a beautiful part of the island—one pretty glade in the vine-draped forest was called "Alice in Wonderland." At last we came out on the shore at Vaitongi Village.

Close by the village the foot of an ancient lava flow juts out into the sea. On the black rocks the trade wind swell breaks in never-ending turmoil.

We induced some of the children of the village to go out on the legendary rock and sing. I saw a small turtle come up in the foaming surf, but the shark did not appear to my vision. But one should not be too critical when investigating old legends. We were told that it was no ordinary turtle and shark that grew old with the passing years, but always a small turtle and a small shark that appeared under the rock of Vaitongi. We walked more than thirty miles that day and came back to Pango Pango after nightfall in a deluge of rain.

Of all strange foods, the Samoans have one of the strangest, and they get that but once a year. The season came around while I was at Pango Pango, and I went out with a party of Samoans after palolos.

It was the night of the twelfth of October when we took a boat and rowed down to the reef near the Village of Utulei.

The palolo is a worm that lives in the coral reefs and comes to the surface once a year, at a certain phase of the moon, the beginning of the last quarter in October. At this particular reef, they would appear just as the moon rose over Mount Peoa, the Rainmaker. As the rising moon lit up the sea, the surface of the water was covered with wriggling, threadlike worms that gave out a pale green phosphorescent light. All about, the natives, in boats and canoes, were scooping them up with improvised hand nets. They ate them raw and wriggling, and put them in pails to take home. In about two hours the run was over.

The palolos develop down in the coral, and at this season they spawn. The palolo breaks in two, and that portion containing the eggs rises to the surface.

I was enjoying my cruise so well that I decided to continue the voyage among the islands of the Western Pacific, instead of returning home by way of Hawaii. There were many alluring islands that I wished to see, but I was more likely to find facilities for overhauling the *Islander* in Fiji.

I was unable to get a chart of the Fiji Group at Pango Pango and had to content myself with a small map, three by four inches in size, from a steamship folder.

VII

Fiji

ON October 23rd the *Islander* beat out of Pango
Pango Harbor and was off for Fiji before a
light northeast wind. I lay a course to pass to the
south of Boscawen Island, intending to sight the place.

Along in the evening, while Tutuila Island was still
in sight, a squall came sweeping down. I reefed the
mainsail, and was reefing the mizzen when the mainsail
gybed over, breaking the boom. The worst of the
blow was soon over, when I set the *Islander* on her
course under jib and mizzen, and went below to sleep
and rest.

The next morning I got out some thin boards that
I had stored in the hold and went to work on the
broken boom. I drove the splintered ends together
the best I could. Then I sawed the boards into narrow
strips about six feet long. These were planed to fit
and well nailed around the broken part, and then rope
lashings put on. It was difficult work with the boat
pitching in the seaway, but when I had the job finished,
the boom seemed as strong as ever.

The weather continued cloudy with rain, and I was
unable to get an observation of the sun. On the evening of the third day out I saw great numbers of

birds, and concluded that I was in the vicinity of Boscawen Island, but the low-hanging clouds and rain obscured the distance. Not being sure of my position, I hove to and waited for daylight. With dawn I sailed away on the course again but never saw the island. The sky cleared about noon when I calculated my position to be southwest and well clear of Boscawen. The wind now came round to southeast with fine clear weather, and I sailed on to the westward.

Wailangilala Island is only a reef with a few coconut trees on it, but there is a lighthouse among the coconut trees, which lies at the entrance of Nanuka Passage, a channel through the reefs of the eastern group of the Fiji Islands.

The sun was setting on October 29th when I sighted the Wailangilala lighthouse. A course was set to run through the passage, and the *Islander* sailed on during the night under the jib and mizzen sails. When morning came there were many islands in sight on either hand. I ran close by Taviuni Island and stood on toward Koro Island, but the wind was light and the sun had set when it was abeam.

During the day I had crossed the one hundred and eightieth meridian, and sailed into east longitude. Although the day before was October 29th this day I wrote October 31st in my log book, and had lost a day.

A lighthouse is a cheerful sight when one is sailing in coral seas. Far too often the reefs are marked with a wreck. My small map was not a very accurate chart, but with the help of the lights and by keeping a close watch, I found my way among the islands and reefs to Suva, on the great Island of Viti Levu.

I came up to the southeast end of Viti Levu in the evening and began to trace the reef that here stands a long way offshore. Night came on with mist and rain. I stood offshore and hove to, and the land was soon lost to view. In the early dawn, a steamer poked her nose out of the drizzle, passed close by, and disappeared in the mist. I felt sure that she was bound for Suva, and followed in her wake. I came up to the reef again, and turned to the westward, looking for an opening. Presently I came to a wreck on the reef, and knew by the sailing directions that it was off Suva Bay. The mist blew away, and I saw the red-roofed houses on the low hills east of the bay.

I found the passage through the reef and sailed into the harbor; then the wind died out, leaving me becalmed, until Harbormaster Twentymen came with a launch and towed the *Islander* to an anchorage off the waterfront. The port doctor came off and found the crew all well. He was closely followed by a reporter, for I was again in the land of the daily newspaper. A few hours later there appeared in *The Pacific Age* of November 2, 1922:

KETCH *ISLANDER* REACHES SUVA

A tiny five-ton ketch made its way through the main passage at Suva amid the rain mists at about ten o'clock this morning, flying an American ensign about the size of a postage stamp, and a quarantine flag.

Captain Twentymen, the Harbormaster, boarded the vessel and piloted her in. The little ship proved to be the *Islander,* and her "crew" Captain H. Pidgeon, the intrepid navigator who is sailing his wee craft single-handed around the world—it is believed for a wager.

When I met Mr. Bach, the government printer, about the first thing he said was, "Well! Let us blow along up home and see if we can find something to eat." And off we went to his big airy bungalow on the hill. As long as I was at Suva, his house was my home.

Mr. Bach, who was something of a photographer himself, placed his darkroom at my disposal and assisted me in making up lantern slides and giving an entertainment, at which I told the people of Suva about my travels. Mr. Bach had lived for many years in Fiji and was able to give me much interesting information about the islands.

The Fiji Group comprises about two hundred and fifty islands of all sizes varying from great mountainous islands with navigable rivers to mere sand cays with a clump of coconut trees. All are surrounded by coral reefs, and far out to sea, where the mountains on the islands are blue in the distance, there are still coral reefs.

There are great areas of fertile soil with many large and productive plantations. There is beautiful scenery on every hand, and the native population, though far from being savages, still keep up many of their interesting customs, and the visitor finds a ready welcome in their picturesque villages.

The residents never tired of telling me of the beauties of Fiji. Some would say that I must not leave Fiji without seeing this or that island, or that some other island was just like fairyland, and then wind up with the injunction, "Now you know this is the hurricane season, and you had better stay right here in the harbor."

The many sailing cutters plying among the islands are all manned by native Fijians. They often came on board to inspect the *Islander*, and to ask questions about my voyage. The Fijians are courageous seamen, but sailing alone they do not comprehend. They said I was a *matai*, which I understood to mean that I was one of the "ancients." Some of them wore red and blue streamers in their hair. These they took off and tied to the *Islander's* main gaff.

One day, when some men were discussing the *Islander*, I heard one of them say, "I don't suppose we will ever hear anything more of the Morrisby boys." A few days later, a small ketch came into the bay and anchored near the *Islander*, and I made the acquaintance of Logan and Rokeby Morrisby, crew of the *Tasman*.

Logan Morrisby had built the *Tasman* in Fiji, and with his brother was just returning from an adventurous cruise to their former home in Sydney, Australia. They had encountered much stormy weather

SCENE ON NAVUA RIVER, VITI LEVU ISLAND, FIJI, WITH THE
ISLANDER AND THE TASMAN.

RESIDENCE OF THE BULI ON BENGA ISLAND, FIJI, WITH THE
GUEST HOUSE AT THE RIGHT.

A TRAFFIC POLICEMAN OF SUVA, FIJI.

THE BULI OF BENGA ISLANDS PRESENTS
THE AUTHOR WITH A BASKET OF DAWAS.

on the return voyage and had been out so long that their friends supposed them to be lost.

There were some facilities at Navua for repairing boats, so when the Morrisbys invited me to come to their home on Navua River, I went along. It was now in the rainy season, and Navua is in the wet district, but when the weather permitted, I busied myself with repairing and repainting the *Islander.*

There was a well-equipped machine shop and a slip for taking boats out of the water at the Navua sugar mill. Mr. Thomas Shayler, the engineer in charge, allowed me to use all the facilities of the place, saying, "You can have anything you want, so long as you leave the mill."

The first thing that I did was to make screens for the cabin of the *Islander,* to exclude the mosquitoes. Along the river these insects came out in swarms after sunset, and without some protection, sleep was out of the question. I made a new main boom, in place of the one that was broken on the way from Samoa, and renewed some of the rigging that had been damaged, probably at the same time the boom was broken. I then took the *Islander* out on the slip and cleaned and painted her throughout.

On week-ends the Morrisbys would often take a party on board the *Tasman,* drop down to the sea, and picnic on one of the small islands or sand cays inside the barrier reef. Here we could fish, swim in the crystal clear water, or sit in the shade of the palms that grow right down to the high water line. But I liked best to hunt for the many varieties of beautiful shells to be found on the coral strand.

One of our excursions was to Benga Island, a Fiji Eden lying a few miles out from Navua River, surrounded by its own maze of coral reefs. The *Buli,* or headman, of the island entertained us with a dinner at his guest house. He set out a large basketful of dawas, saying that they were for me. The Fijians prize the dawa above all other fruits. I have never seen them elsewhere. They look much like large plums and are very sweet to the taste. Whether it was native etiquette for me to eat the lot, I did not know, but as there was a bushel or more of the dawas, I shared them with the rest of the party.

One day, after I had returned to Suva, I met Harbormaster Twentymen, and he said to me, "There is a hurricane between Samoa and Fiji, and it is coming this way." He advised me to take the *Islander* over to Mosquito Harbor, a small cove behind some islands at the west end of Suva Bay. There I would be comparatively safe, even in a hurricane.

It was about four o'clock in the afternoon when I started to sail over. I was not well acquainted with the channel, and ran aground near the entrance to the harbor. I put one of the anchors in the skiff and carried it out into deeper water, but the tide was falling fast, and when I had the anchor run out, it was too late to kedge off. All I could do was to wait for the incoming tide.

I could not have got in a much worse place to await

the coming of a hurricane. Night was coming on with rain, and the wind was rising. At low tide the *Islander* listed far over on her side, and I perched on her sloping deck, hoping that the hurricane would not strike. It was about ten o'clock when the tide had risen, and after some hard work at the windlass, the *Islander* was floated off. I then found that the anchor was foul of something, and I could not raise it. After buoying the end of the chain I let it slip and sailed in behind the islands, where the water was quite smooth and the wind almost entirely cut off. After all, the hurricane passed some other way, and I was glad that it did not strike while I was sticking on the spit. At low tide the next day, I went out and recovered my anchor, which was found to be hooked in a hole in the coral.

With the coming of the good weather season, I made ready to sail for the New Hebrides Islands. I was unable to get a chart of the New Hebrides in Suva but found one of the Southwest Pacific and one of Torres Strait.

One of my friends, Bob Smith, gave me the parting advice, "See all the world, and then come back to settle in Fiji."

VIII

New Hebrides

ON April 25, 1923, the *Islander* stood out to sea
with her bowsprit pointing westward once more.
The wind was light, and it was the morning of the
fourth day out when the last peaks of Fiji disappeared.

On the eighth day out the wind came up strong with
a rain squall, raising a rough sea. It blew stronger
after sunset, and the rising sea tossed wildly, but I
made good time all night with only the jib and mizzen
sail set.

The sky had cleared in the evening, and the moon
came up bright, making a wonderful sight as the boat
bounded over the foaming sea. To me, there is something weird and beautiful about the sea in the moonlight. I scarcely know how long it was that I sat
there in the companionway contemplating the wonder
of it all, the *Islander* keeping the course all the while
with no one at the helm. It was far into the night
when I went below and slept, while the *Islander* rose
and fell with the billows and sailed on and on into
the west.

When I came on deck at daylight, I was surprised
to see land on the starboard bow. It was Efate Island,
and I had been coming up to it faster than I had

thought. Far away to the south I could see the peaks of Eromanga. But the wind died out to a faint breeze, and the sun had set when I entered beautiful Meli Bay, where the *Islander* drifted about on the quiet waters all night.

With the coming of daylight, I was up making the best of an offshore breeze and made my way up the bay to Vila and dropped the anchor alongside H. M. Yacht *Euphrosyne*. As soon as the health official had paid his visit, Commander Barrett of the *Euphrosyne* came on board and invited me to come on board the yacht for lunch.

The scene all around was charming, and soon I had made friends with British and French. A French resident, Plain Le Mescam, who kept me provided with fruit and vegetables, took me for a drive into the country to see his plantation. I was astonished at the amount of arable land on the island, and the wonderful fertility of the soil. Coconuts, cocoa, and coffee were the principal crops grown, but fruit and vegetables all do well. About all the cultivation anything gets is to have the jungle and weeds cut down and the rats poisoned. The two common complaints of the settlers were the fever and the Condominium government, and they did not seem to entertain any hope of relief from either. In the New Hebrides, for the first time in the South Seas, I came to a land where few of the inhabitants were free from the fever. Aside from this, I think I should find it a pleasant place to live.

I went with Mr. Raff, superintendent of schools, to visit a community living on a small island in Meli Bay, who were the descendants of Polynesian castaways. While making a voyage in one of their seagoing canoes, a party had drifted away in a storm and were unable to regain their homes. They finally reached Efate, where they seized the little island and made it their stronghold. They intermarried with the Efate natives and obtained a foothold on the main island, where they now have small farms and gardens. They speak a Polynesian dialect, and many of them have the straight hair of their Polynesian ancestors. I was shown a large piece of iron, which they said had been used as an anchor on the great canoe in which their forefathers had come to the island. This emigration had taken place since the first Europeans came to the South Seas, but it is probable that many of the Pacific islands were peopled in the same way.

On another island in the bay was a village of civilized New Hebrides natives. I went to call on the chief, who showed me with pride a diploma from a missionary school. The next day he brought me a basket of oranges, saying, "I bring them to you for coming so far to see us." The civilized natives of New Hebrides were more respectful to the whites than any other black people I have seen, and I was told they were honest.

Along the shores of the larger islands of New Hebrides there are many small islands; and these are the favorite places for the villages of the natives.

There being fewer mosquitoes on the small islands, it is more comfortable and healthier to live there. The British hospital for New Hebrides is located on an island in Meli Bay. The jungle has been cleared away so that the wind can sweep the island, and it is said that no one contracts the fever there.

In many places I have seen brilliant phosphorescent displays in the water at night. In Meli Bay, for the first time, I noticed a marine creature swimming that leaves a phosphorescent streak behind, and when one of them stops for a time, the water all around becomes phosphorescent. On one occasion the surface of the bay was a multitude of phosphorescent streaks ten to fifteen feet in length.

Wishing to see something of the more primitive natives of the New Hebrides, I decided to call at one of the northern islands, before sailing for New Guinea. I gathered what local information I could at Vila, and Commander Barrett gave me a chart of the northern islands of the group.

On the afternoon of May 21st, the *Islander* glided out of beautiful Meli Bay. Outside the bay was a small, green island that looked for all the world like a broad-brimmed hat thrown on the sea. Taking my departure from Hat Island, I sailed on through the night. At daylight Epi Island was abeam, and on the starboard bow a great cloud of smoke rose from the crater of Ambrym Island. Then as the sun came up, Malekula Island appeared out of the haze on the port beam. All day I coasted along the shore of

Malekula, and the sun shone red through the dust drifting out from Ambrym.

When the sun was low, I ran in behind a small outlying island looking for an anchorage, as I was tired. Seeing that the water was protected by the island and the reef, I headed the *Islander* in toward a sandy beach. At that moment some of the wildest looking men that I ever saw running naked pushed a canoe into the water and came straight for my ship. Their appearance was startling, to say the least. I suddenly remembered that the first officer of the *Euphrosyne* had told me that it was not safe for a man to be sailing alone on that coast. Dressed only in bark belts, and grinning like fiends they boarded the *Islander*. Well! I grinned too. Grinning still, they directed me to an anchorage close to the beach in front of their village. There was a board house among the trees. I pointed to it and said, "Missionary stop."

One of my visitors answered, "No, him finish," but I did not understand enough of their talk to learn how he finished. After all, appearances are deceptive, and they were all very friendly. Two more canoe loads came off, but our conversation was mostly limited to handshakes and smiles, and when I made a move to prepare my supper, they went on shore, and only two came back to bring me a cake of *lap-lap* (native bread, made of grated yams and coconuts).

I was off with the dawn and two hours' sailing brought me to Atchin Island. When I was leaving

Vila, Mr. Raff had asked me to call on the Nicholsons at Atchin. As I came under the lee of the island near the mission house, a wild looking crew came off and assisted me in anchoring and furling the sails. I found that I could carry on a limited conversation with many of them in *bêche de mer* English. After I had entertained my visitors for a time, a boy came off with an invitation for me to call at the mission.

At the mission I found Mrs. Nicholson and Mrs. Smith, who with Mrs. Smith's little son were the only white people on the island. Mr. Nicholson and Mr. Smith were away on Ambrym Island building a new mission house, and the two courageous women were carrying on at the lonely outpost by themselves. They were glad to get news, and I was equally interested in hearing them tell of their life and work among the savages. The Atchin people had recently had a fight with the natives of another island, when they killed a man, and it was believed that they had eaten him. But they said the natives did not steal, and that I need have no fear of their molesting anything of mine. The next day they went with me to visit the natives in their villages.

Atchin Island is small and densely wooded. Scattered about amid sylvan scenes were the little thatched huts where the men of Atchin kept their wives and pigs, and I was not always sure which huts were for the wives or which were for the pigs. The men lived apart in clubhouses or barracks, where they prepared their own food, for the men of Atchin did not eat with women. The New Hebrides natives are not so large and showy as their Fijian neighbors, nor have they the wonderful hair or independent bearing of the Fijians, but many of the Atchin men have the well-developed figures of men used to fighting their battles with primitive weapons.

The most interesting place on the island was the ground where the people carried out their strange religious rites, for they were heathens and clung stubbornly to their old traditions. They called their place of worship a *hamil*. At the edge of a clearing in the forest was a large banyan tree. In its shade stood the big wooden drums that were used for calling up the spirits. The tops of the drums had grotesque faces carved on them, to which were attached the jaws of pigs that had been sacrificed on the hamil. What spirits or deities the faces represented I did not find out, but Mrs. Nicholson called the strange rites held on the hamil devil worship.

After night had fallen, I made my way back to the hamil ground, guided by the sound of the big drums. Some twenty or more men were stamping up and down before the drums in a sort of torchlight procession and singing a chantey of three or four words over and over again. Surging around them was a ring of young girls holding hands, their faces streaked with red paint and answering the words of the men with a wild chant of their own. In the dim flickering light of the torches the hamil was a weird uncanny place. At these night séances some of the old men claimed

ON THE HAMIL GROUND, ATCHIN ISLAND, NEW HEBRIDES,
WHERE THE IDOLS ARE FESTOONED WITH THE JAWS OF PIGS.

MEN OF ATCHIN ISLAND ON THE HAMIL GROUND.

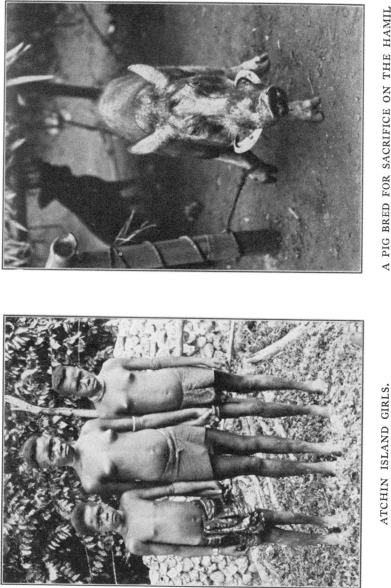

A PIG BRED FOR SACRIFICE ON THE HAMIL GROUND.

ATCHIN ISLAND GIRLS.

to see the ghosts of the dead perched on the branches of the trees round about.

As I was watching the strange scene, an old man, wearing a cast-off hat, came and sat down by my side, his face beaming friendliness. He addressed me with so much intelligence, that I inquired where he had learned to talk English. He said, "Me been Brisbane ten years, work sugar plantation." They had made a law in Australia, "No more black fella." Then they had brought him home. I asked him what the dancers were saying. He said they were only talking dog talk, "No words, only bark like dog," and gave no other explanation. He told me at some length about the Australian "black fella," whom he said had "No pig; no house," and at night lay down by the side of the road to sleep. While we were talking, one of the small boys who were sitting around us went to sleep. The old man said it was his pickaninny, and he must take him to his house. Tenderly he took up the sleeping child and left the hamil. The torches of the dancers were dying out, and the séance ended. Silently the spectators crept away in the night, and by some instinct I found my way through the dark woods to the shore.

Some of the clans of Atchin were staging a "revival" of their old rites as a last stand against the efforts of the missionaries. I came across a gang of stalwart men dragging some heavy logs of wood to an old hamil ground that was being repaired. There were four of the logs, which with incredible labor had been brought from far in the interior of Malekula Island. The logs were to be carved into new drums, and no suitable wood for the purpose was to be found on Atchin. Long ropelike vines were attached to the logs, and many strong hands moved them along to the sound of much puffing and blowing. My old friend from Brisbane was acting as water boy and carried along a supply of green coconuts for the refreshment of the workers. There was some special sanctity about this work, and each had a tuft of green leaves stuck in his belt at the rear. When the logs were finally landed on the hamil ground, a fence or screen of coconut branches was built all around, for the carving of the drums was a tabu process, and no one might watch the workman at the mysterious task.

One day I went to the hamil where I had seen the night dance. The people were gathering there with large quantities of yams and ten or a dozen pigs. It was the ceremony of consecrating the food for a feast.

An old man seized a heavy chunk of wood with both hands and beat a furious tattoo on one of the drums. This I presumed was for the purpose of calling up the spirit that the drum represented. The pigs were led or dragged by a thong attached to a front foot, and tied to a post in front of the drums. The yams were brought forward and arrayed conspicuously. Many of the fine large ones were tied to the end of bamboo poles and decorated with streamers of coconut leaves. When everything was arranged to the satisfaction of the master of ceremonies, the drum was beaten and all retired to a distance and sat down. For a few minutes they waited in silence with the display before the drums. Then some men came forward and dragged the pigs close in front of the drums where they were rapped over the head with a club. Some of the pigs seemed to be done for entirely, but others were only stunned and recovered to be led away to the ovens. However, they must all be ceremonially killed before the drums. There was one beautiful white pig that only received a light tap that did not bring a squeal. I was told that he was preserved to be ceremonially presented at every feast. After the ceremony was over, the pigs and yams were distributed among the people and the crowd dispersed. One of the old men who officiated came to me with a bunch of yams and said, "Him yam belong a you," then he called a boy to take them to my boat.

Displayed on the hamil ground, some of them attached to the drums, were the jaws of hundreds of pigs that had been sacrificed there. Many of the jaws had long tusks, some of which had grown in a curve until they formed two complete circles. It seemed that when a pig was presented for a feast, the owner received credit according to the size of its tusks. For this reason the natives sometimes broke out the upper tusks of a pig; then the lower tusks, having nothing to oppose them, grew out like a ram's horns. An intelligent young man took me to see one of these pigs that was being kept for its tusks. The owner kept the pig confined in a pen and tied to a post, to prevent him from breaking his tusks fighting with other pigs. This pig's tusks had completed one turn, entered his jaws and come out again, and was well started on a second turn. They said it took about seven years for a pig to grow tusks with two turns, when it was time to sacrifice him before he died of old age.

The people lived and kept their pigs on Atchin, but their gardens were located on the mainland of Malekula. Each morning the women folks crossed over the channel to work in the fields, and came back in the evening laden with the yams that were their principal food. One morning I rowed across to Malekula. A big native met me on the beach and tried to converse with me without much success, but I understood that he wished me to go somewhere with him. We crossed a stream and entered the forest. When we came to a thicket of wild banana plants, where the trail seemed like a tunnel, it occurred to me that it was a strange place to be following a naked savage, about whom lurked a suspicion of cannibalism. But at last we came out into a clearing, where a woman was working in a yam patch, and three or four healthy pickaninnies played in the dirt. It was his field and he wanted me to see it. When I was ready to return, he tied up a bunch of yams for me and came with me to Atchin. There was too much swell on the Malekula shore for launching the dinghy with both of us in it, but the native managed it by wading out through the breakers and lifting the bow to the swells. The New Hebrides natives excel in the cultivation of yams. These are of superior quality to any I have seen elsewhere. Some that I procured from the Atchin natives kept in perfect condition until I used the last of them near four months later.

Yaws are prevalent throughout the tropical islands, but these infectious sores are more common in the malarial region of the western Pacific. It was rare to see an Atchin native that was not scarred, and some were loathsome with offensive sores. My only personal experience with yaws was in the Marquesas, when a neglected abrasion developed into an ulcer that finally healed after repeated applications of potassium permanganate solution. After this experience I treated all cuts and abrasions with a solution of potassium permanganate and water which never failed to end any infection.

IX

New Guinea

ON the morning of May 29th, the *Islander's* sails were once more spread to the breeze, and I was off. Running before a light east wind, I passed through Bougainville Strait and lay a course west by north. As soon as I was clear of Malekula Island, a heavy swell set in from the south. A gale blew up from the east, starting cross seas that gave the *Islander* a most uncomfortable roll. Cooking utensils and gear broke loose and went sliding about. The large water cask shifted from its fastenings, but firewood and other articles jammed around it kept it from doing damage. During my whole voyage I do not remember to have met up with such a disagreeable and long-continued twisting motion as the meeting of these two swells worked up.

For several days I ran under close reefed sails; then the wind and seas went down so that the *Islander* was almost becalmed. This gave me a chance to go aloft and reeve in a new lift for the main boom in place of one that had broken during the gale. A light wind came up from the southeast, and I changed the course to northwest to bring up to the New Guinea coast.

Sunday, June 10th, was a memorable day on board the *Islander,* for on that day I sighted land beyond the Pacific Ocean. Soon after sunrise low islands were seen on the starboard beam, and a few hours later the cloud-capped mountains of New Guinea appeared. During the day I sailed by many small islands, and before sunset came up to South Cape.

My chart of the Southwest Pacific did not show local features of the New Guinea coast, and I had no sailing directions, so I approached the mainland beyond South Cape cautiously, looking for reefs, but saw none. I came close up to the shore under Cloudy Mountain, where the land sloped abruptly down to the sea, but saw no sign of inhabitants.

Standing offshore a little, I sailed slowly along with a light breeze until morning when I was off Eagle Point. During the day the *Islander* drifted by Orangerie Bay almost becalmed, and the sun was hot. I saw smoke rising from several fires on the shore, and far above were the mountains rising to majestic heights.

With no charts or sailing directions and having no local knowledge of the coast, it would have been wise to give the place a wide berth. But there was a strange fascination in this land with its lofty cloud-capped mountains.

The next morning I awoke to see two islands astern, and whether I passed between them or to one side I did not know. A little later I met a Papuan double canoe, its crab-claw sail swaying to the offshore breeze and a naked Papuan at the steering paddle. We passed close by but neither of us spoke, and I think I was the more astonished of the two. As soon as I was through gazing at the Papuan sailor and his strange craft, I looked ahead and saw breakers dashing the white water high in air. I had come up to the barrier reef that from this point stretches along the New Guinea shore. Over the reef, in a green lagoon, I could see Papuan canoes sailing about. I sailed along off the reef until the next day at noon, when I came to a long low point of land planted to coconut trees. At the end of the point, and just inside the reef, was a Papuan village built out over the water on piles, and among the trees on the point were a few European houses. This place I recognized as Hood Point.

Now when I was at Vila, I had met a former resident of Port Moresby, New Guinea. As I had not been able to get charts of New Guinea, I inquired how I should know when I came to Port Moresby, where I intended calling. His instructions were to close up with the New Guinea shore at Hood Point, and then coast along, keeping a close lookout. When I should see European houses on a hill, that would be Port Moresby, as there were no other houses along that part of the coast.

A good breeze was blowing from the southeast, and I ran on before it. Along in the evening I saw houses on a hill and concluded that Port Moresby was near. It was now too late to attempt finding my way into a strange reef-bound harbor, so I lowered the mainsail and headed the *Islander* up into the wind, intending to cruise slowly around in the vicinity until morning. I went below and was preparing my evening meal, when I heard a harsh grating sound that would have filled any seafaring man with alarm. Springing out, I saw white coral all around, although there were no breakers in sight and I was several miles from the land. Apparently I had come up under the lee of a reef, and as there was about five feet of water over it, there were no breakers to indicate its presence. There was only a slight swell running, but with each undulation the *Islander* slid farther onto the reef, and there came the sound of the iron-shod keel on the coral.

The *Islander* was not fast on the reef, possibly she would have gone on over it, but I was able to wear her around on the other tack and headed off. She grated a few more times, then I saw the white coral going from under and she was soon in deep water, but I had lost my appetite for supper, and I stood offshore all night long.

When morning came I was a long way out, but I soon made out Mount Astrolabe and the supposed location of Port Moresby. The wind was light, and it was near noon before I came up to the reef again. I found an opening through the reef, and after much winding about among small islands and shoals, I finally came to a wharf near the head of an inlet. Here I found out that I was in Bootless Inlet, where a copper mine was being opened up, and that Port Moresby was a few miles farther along the coast. The buildings on the hill had been erected since my acquaintance at Vila had left the country. In the evening a half-caste man came out on the wharf and startled me by singing, "Just Before the Battle, Mother."

Anchored in the quiet inlet that night, I had a good sleep which I was greatly in need of. The next morning, after getting a little instruction, I beat out of the inlet and sailed along in the sheltered water behind the barrier reef to Port Moresby, where I came to anchor at noon on June 15th.

A motor boat had arrived from Bootless Inlet earlier in the day with news of my coming, and a few white men had gathered at the landing to see the stranger who was sailing alone on their coast. Some surprise was expressed when they learned that I had found my way into Bootless Inlet and out again without charts or sailing directions. Mr. Percival Leigh, the only American resident, welcomed me with an invitation to call on him for any assistance I should need while in port.

During my several days' stay at the little town, I was well entertained by the Leighs, Grimshaws, Armitts and others. Mr. Murcutt, a young Australian, took such a fancy to the *Islander* that he copied the plan with the intention of constructing a boat on her lines.

Port Moresby is built on a wind-swept point, and

is a healthy place compared to the region at its back door, where clouds and mists hang continually and the people coming in from outlying districts complained of the fever. That the trade winds blow strong here I had reason to know a few days after my arrival.

I had been spending an evening ashore with friends, entertaining them with photographs, and listening to tales of savages and cannibals. I started for my ship at about eleven o'clock, thinking of what a wonderful thing it was to be alive. It was a dark night and the wind was blowing a gale right offshore. I got in my dinghy and rowed out in the darkness, but there was no *Islander*. She had gone on a cruise by herself, leaving me on the beach with only the clothes I stood in and a book of photographs under my arm.

I woke up my friends, Murcutt and Leigh, and they borrowed the government launch in which we cruised out over the bay looking for the lost *Islander,* but it was a wild night and too dark, and there was danger of piling the launch up on the reefs, so we had to go back and wait for daylight. With the first streaks of dawn we were off again. Far out we found the *Islander* anchored to a reef. The chain was laid out across the reef, and she was swinging to it in the quiet water under the lee. How she could have gotten by the reef without striking, I could not see, but apparently no damage had been done, and articles that I had left sitting on the cabin table were still in place. When we hauled in the anchor we found the stock broken out. We concluded that the stock had caught on some obstruction when it was put down at the anchorage, preventing the anchor from biting into the bottom. The stock must have broken under the strain of the fierce gusts that swept over the harbor in the early part of the night, and the *Islander* drifted away in the darkness with her broken anchor until it caught in the jagged coral. The *Islander* was brought back to the anchorage, and then in Mr. Leigh's machine shop we made a new stock for the anchor. I had had a bad night, but it all ended well.

On the shore of the bay, near Port Moresby, is the large native village of Hanauabada, whose inhabitants are a maritime race. Their racing canoes may be classed among the swiftest sailing craft in the world, and as a result of the week-end regattas held at Port Moresby much cash changes hands among the white residents. The canoe is a dugout thirty to forty feet in length, to which is attached an outrigger of light wood. The racing canoes are equipped with two masts, each carrying a large square sprit sail that is now made out of canvas. When the wind is strong the crew go out on the outrigger and balance with their weight the pressure of the wind on the sail. The peculiar thing about the sailing of these canoes is that on either tack the outrigger is always kept up to windward. When the canoe goes about, the sheets are hauled to the other end of the canoe and the helmsman runs to that end with the steering paddle, and they are off with bow and stern reversed. Behind the barrier reef that stretches along the coast of New Guinea there

HANAUABADA, A PAPUAN VILLAGE NEAR PORT MORESBY, NEW GUINEA.

A CANOE RACE AT PORT MORESBY.

The sailing canoes of New Guinea are among the swiftest wind borne craft in the world.

MEN OF HALL SOUND, NEW GUINEA.

A TATTOOED GIRL OF NEW GUINEA.

are many sheltered waterways; however, the canoes are remarkably seaworthy. Several of the larger canoes are lashed together into a sort of sailing raft, called a *lakatoi,* and in these the seamen of Hanauabada make long trading voyages, carrying pottery, stoneware, and other articles manufactured in the village for barter with the natives of other localities.

There is always a fascination in seeing the homes of strange people, and I found Hanauabada especially interesting. The youngsters always seem to sight a stranger as soon as one appears on the horizon, and a merry troop of boys and girls gather to escort one about their village. I should like to have understood their talk, for they kept up a continual round of good-natured banter among themselves. There was no superfluous clothing among this crowd. The girls were becomingly arrayed in grass skirts and the smaller boys in nothing at all. I do not remember to have seen a native in the village wearing white man's togs, and I am under the impression that the administration of Papua forbids the natives to wear the tatters of civilization. Some of the young girls were decorated with bits of tattooing, for among the Papuans it is the women who are tattooed, and as it is a very painful process they begin while the subject is young and add to the design from time to time. Many of the women were elaborately tattooed from head to foot.

Originally, no doubt, the salt water people built their

houses on stakes over the sea, as a protection against the raids of the bush natives. Although there is now no danger from this source, the construction seems well adapted to a people who spend so much of their time in canoes, and it solves many sanitary problems. Not only do the men of Hanauabada follow the sea in their canoes, but they make up the crews of the trading vessels that ply along the coast. Following in the wake of their elders, the boys of the village were busy building and sailing model canoes.

On June 27th, I sailed out through the winding passage among the reefs and gained the open sea on my way to Yule Island, at the entrance to Hall Sound, where I wished to call before leaving New Guinea. The wind was light, and night found me off Redscar Bay, some miles from my destination, so I hove to and waited for morning. The wind began to breeze up, and I spent a most uncomfortable night, with the *Islander* plunging into a short, steep sea.

A gale was blowing at dawn, and I stood off on the course under short sail. I don't remember to have seen a more vicious sea than was being kicked up, as if we were crossing a bar. One spiteful comber broke on the stern, and for a moment we were lost in a cloud of spray. I soon made out Yule Island and the white billows breaking high over the long point that stands far out on the opposite side of the entrance to Hall Sound. On rounding the point a clear passage opened out, so I put on more sail and ran in.

Seeing a ketch anchored under the point on the

southeast side of the sound, I ran up alongside and dropped the anchor.

The water seemed shallow, but the native skipper of the ketch said there was a fathom and a half. Being tired and sleepy I turned into my berth. I was awakened when the keel began pounding on the bottom. The tide had fallen and the swell coming in through the entrance was dropping my boat on the hard ground with a heavy jar. The crew of the ketch had gone on shore. I got the anchor up and put on sail, but the yawl was too hard on bottom to come about and drifted off to leeward thumping the ground with every swell. Several times the rudder struck with such violence that I thought it would be driven up through the boat. After bumping along for about two hundred yards we went off into deeper water when I anchored and went to sleep again. I was awakened again by a commotion, and found that the crew of the ketch had returned and were going through the same experience that I had had. When they had gotten off into deeper water, I questioned them about the anchorage in the sound and learned that there was a sheltered harbor behind Yule Island. They had come to this point to take on rock for ballast. It was now after sunset but after getting what directions I could from them, I sailed around to the leeward of Yule Island and came to anchor near where I could see a light on shore.

Yule Island is the headquarters of the fathers of the Sacred Heart Mission, who have established a number of mission stations extending into the far interior of New Guinea. The magistrate of the district resides here and there is a receiving station for a plantation on the mainland. It was close by the buildings of this latter place that I had anchored. Mr. Thomas Baker, the man in charge of the station, came off early in the morning to extend the hospitality of the place and to invite me over for breakfast. Later we went to call on the magistrate, Aliston Blyth, and his wife and had lunch with them.

The magistrate was holding court that afternoon, and around his bungalow office was gathered a crowd of strange bushy-headed natives whose attire consisted for the most part of ornaments and flowers. They had come over from the mainland for the purpose of settling, before the magistrate, some trouble they had gotten into among themselves. But for the white man's law, it would probably have been settled with one crowd wiping the other out. For all their wild appearance they were amiable enough and were quite willing to pose for a photograph when the matter was explained to them by one of the native constables.

One of the fathers showed me around the mission grounds. At the mission school the sister in charge had the children do some exercises for me. They sang, "Just Before the Battle, Mother," and I remembered the young half-caste man I had heard singing this song at Bootless Inlet. No doubt he had been educated in this school. A special interest was taken at this school in caring for little half-caste waifs.

The next morning Mr. Baker sent Gabriel, a Burmese workman, and a crew of Papuans over to the mainland to get logs from the woods near Delana Village. I went along with them. While we were crossing, Gabriel, whose wife was a Papuan, told me that the natives had a remarkable way of communicating with each other from long distances. It was a mystery to him, but he said his wife's people, who lived far inland, were informed immediately about happenings in his family. Hard luck for Gabriel.

At Delana I found Mr. Dauncey, an English missionary who had resided in Papua for thirty-five years. I enjoyed my visit with this intelligent man, who besides his fund of information about the Papuans, was interested in photography and yachting, and these we discussed over some recent numbers of the *Rudder* that I found among his books and papers. Leaving Mr. Dauncey busy attending to the afflictions of his flock who came to him with their sores, I went to see the natives in the village. They were a strange but good-natured lot. One might have supposed they were made up for some sort of pantomime. Many of them seemed to have individual taste in the matter of adorning themselves with feathers and flowers, but a young man of Hall Sound is not fully dressed until he has coated himself from head to foot with some cosmetic, apparently coconut oil and red clay. I found no one in the village that I could converse with, but one intelligent man took a great interest in my camera, and when I had shown him how to push the button, he exposed a plate while I was standing among the crowd. The result demonstrated that I sometimes found myself in some funny places.

When I tired of strolling about the village, I paused in the shade of a tree to watch a woman making clay water jars. From somewhere the friendly natives brought out a canvas chair, the work of some white man, and placed it in the shade, for me to sit on. The woman roughly shaped the jar out of rather stiff clay, and then a smooth stone was passed round the inside while it was beaten on the outside with a wooden paddle until it was of the required shape and thickness.

My attention was attracted to a man chewing betel nuts. He came and sat down near me with a large bunch of green nuts, fresh from the tree, and chewed up one nut after another until a dozen or more had been consumed. By that time he appeared drowsy and went and slung a hammock under his house and lay down. The betel nut palm grows in profusion throughout New Guinea, and most Papuans are addicted to chewing a mixture of betel nut and coral lime. The betel nut is about as palatable as a bitter acorn, and the addition of the lime may neutralize the bitter, acrid taste.

As evening came on, Gabriel's crew, who were waiting for the tide to float the heavily laden boat, built a fire on the shore. I went to where they were, and as there was still some time to wait, the simple, kindly people brought their canvas chair and placed it by the fire for me. When the tide was in, the silent Papuan boatmen took up their oars, and once more I came back to Yule Island in the moonlight.

It would have been a pleasure to have lingered in this wonderland of beautiful scenery and strange people, but I was expecting letters at Thursday Island; so after a few days around Yule Island, I sailed out of Hall Sound and stood away for the Bligh Entrance to Torres Strait.

X

Torres Strait

I SAILED from Yule Island on July 1st. The day was fair, with a light southeast wind blowing.

One wishes for good weather when passing through Torres Strait, and at this time of the year might expect it, but on the afternoon of the second day out the sky clouded up and the wind blew hard, raising a choppy sea in the shallow waters. I should have hove to and waited for morning, but instead I ran on under short sail and began watching for Bramble Cay and Darnley Island.

Morning came with mist and rain, and for most of the day I was lost in a maze of reefs and sand cays. I had a chart of Torres Strait, but the weather was too thick for me to see the landmarks. I saw some Papuan canoes and tried to come up with them, but they sailed into shallow water near a line of rocks on the edge of a great mud flat. The mist lifted somewhat and I made out my position to be between Bristow Island and the Warrior Reefs, but the day was far spent and night was coming on when I began to beat out to gain the open stretch of water to the eastward, and Bristow Island and the sand cays faded out in the darkness. At two o'clock I hove to, but all through the night I listened for the sound of breakers.

July 4th dawned with no land in sight, but out of the southeast an occasional squall swept down on us. I got up the mainsail and headed south, looking for islands. I ran into quiet water, and found that I was in the lee of two small cays, but so thick was the weather that the first I saw of them was the white coral under the keel. They were laid down on the chart, and from them I lay a course for Dalrymple Island. In about two hours coconut trees were showing through the mist. I ran close by, and when I was sure it was Dalrymple I stood on a course to pick up Rennell Island.

I came up to Rennell Island at noon and ran close by the shore till I saw the white sand underneath and let the anchor go. I was tired with constant watching and the loss of two nights' sleep, but I saw people watching from the shore, so I got out the dinghy and went over. There I met Tom Savage and his family. They owned the island and turned out the best it afforded for me. After I had eaten, I went for a walk and found the island a wonderful place. Like many others in Torres Strait, it was just a reef with a sand bank on it crowned with coconut trees. There were nautilus shells and cuttle bone strewn all along the shore and beautiful shells everywhere on the beach. Out beyond, where the falling tide had left the reef bare, a troop of great white pelicans with black wings stalked gravely about. Sea gulls, that I had not seen in the South Sea islands, were flying about.

I had cut my hand while husking a coconut on the way over from Yule Island, and it was now inflamed with some kind of New Guinea infection and very painful. If I was to save my thumb, something had to be done, so I went on board and spent the rest of the day and most of the night soaking my hand in hot water and permanganate. So ended July 4, 1923.

My hand was still sore the next day, and I was tired all over, so I stayed at Rennell Island and enjoyed the hospitality of the Savage family. Tom's mother gathered leaves to bind on my sore hand. They brought out the pretty shells they had gathered and gave me all I would take. Tom gave me a splendid pair of gold-lipped pearl shells, and his sister a pretty pandanus basket to carry the shells in. They came out and admired the *Islander,* and Tom said she was stronger than any boat in Torres Strait. The next morning, when I sailed, they ransacked their garden for green corn, sweet potatoes, and pumpkins for me to use on my journey. They came to the shore and bade me an affectionate farewell, and as I sailed away into the west, a rain squall swept down and blotted Rennell Island and its people from my sight.

In the same squall a strop on the main gaff parted, and the mainsail came down, but I kept on my way under jib and mizzen. I passed by Arden and Aured Islands, and in the afternoon anchored in the lee of Coconut Island, where a large ketch had also taken shelter. I went on shore where there was a small village. The people, who appeared to be Torres

Strait natives, were amusing themselves with a game similar to quoits. Sitting down in the sand, they tossed the large smooth seeds of a tree and tried to have them stop on mats placed at either end of the pitch. I did not understand their talk and soon went on board to rest, but far into the night I heard the natives drumming and singing around a fire on shore.

A gale with passing squalls was blowing the next morning, but I tied in reefs and sailed on toward Thursday Island. It was a wet day of dodging reefs and rocks in a rough choppy sea, and the landmarks were so obscured that I had difficulty in keeping the course. Night had fallen before I reached my destination, but in the darkness I came up under Tuesday Islets and dropped the anchor. The next morning I ran in through a reef-strewn channel and anchored at Thursday Island. That same day the sky cleared, and for the rest of my stay in Torres Strait the weather was fine. Residents of Thursday Island told me that the stormy weather of the last few days was very unusual for Torres Strait in the month of July.

Thursday Island had a dry, bleak appearance when I saw it. I was told the annual rainfall was about seventy inches, but that it falls in torrents during the season of western monsoons, washing most of the soil off, and leaving the stones and gravel. The prosperity of the place depends largely on the pearl fisheries, and much of that business has now gone to Broome and Port Darwin, which probably accounts for the number of empty and deserted houses. I believe Thursday

Island once boasted of having the largest pile of empty tin cans in the world, but I imagine that some other locality can now claim to have a larger.

It is astonishing the size and number of papers that have to be made out and signed at the customhouse, before a ship of the *Islander's* small tonnage can enter Australia. Lists of all stores had to be filed in triplicate both coming and going, but the officials were very nice to me and made the process as painless as possible.

Thursday Island is a sort of crossroads of the sea, where I could go south behind the Barrier Reef to visit the cities of Australia, or pass through the East Indies to the Philippine Islands, but I finally decided to return to California by way of the Cape of Good Hope and the Panama Canal. Here I came onto the route of Captain Joshua Slocum, who passed through Torres Strait in June, 1897, when he sailed alone around the world in the sloop *Spray*. From this point the *Islander* was to follow closely on the track of the *Spray* to the West Indies.

The *Islander* was in need of repairs and paint, for she had scraped on many a reef since coming off the ways in Fiji. The tide runs strong through the anchorage at Thursday Island, and it is exposed to the sweep of the trade wind, a combination which makes things disagreeable on board a small boat; so I moved over to a quiet cove in the lee of Prince of Wales Island to do the work.

While I was busy at this task, the American yacht

Ohio called in at Thursday Island. Hearing that I was there, the owner, E. W. Scripps, sent his launch over to the cove with an invitation for me to come on board. Mayor Corwin, of Thursday Island, was also a guest of the Scripps party that evening. The *Ohio* had been cruising around Japan and the Philippines and had come last from Surabaya in Java. There were some arguments about the relations between the United States and Japan, and Mayor Corwin discussed Australian politics, but Mr. Scripps' interest was centered on the small sum of money required for a cruise in the *Islander*. I did not enlighten him much on the subject, but he calculated that it did not cost me more than fifty cents a day. I suppose he had conducted business on a pretty close margin himself in his younger days. From the bright lights of the beautiful yacht I returned to my scraper and paint brush.

The tides in Torres Strait are peculiar and depend much on the declination of the moon and the wind. With the full moon tide, I beached the *Islander* to clean and paint the bottom. There were some repairs to be done on the keel and rudder, but with a piece of hardwood spiked on the keel, a little cement, and a good coat of copper paint over all, the *Islander* was fit as ever. The sails were now showing the effects of the climate and long wear, and they came in for a lot of work. There was an old abandoned house on the shore close by, the veranda of which I turned into a sail loft.

In the rear of the house I found a well of fresh water, and I availed myself of the supply to finish some photographs. On account of the heat, much of this work had to be done at night, and with the difficulties encountered while working in my small cabin, I wondered that I got any results at all. I also cut a supply of firewood. There were bees in the tree that I cut for wood, and I had honey. The bees were very small and stingless. They stored their acid-sweet honey in small round cells that much resembled fish eggs. I was told that bees were plentiful, and the honey much sought for by the Australian blacks.

When I had finished with the work, I returned to Thursday Island and was making preparations to sail when I heard of the death of President Harding. When the message was received at Thursday Island, Mayor Corwin placed the flag over the town hall at half mast, and then came to tell me.

XI

Indian Ocean

ON August 7, 1923, I sailed from Thursday Island for Timor. It was three-thirty in the afternoon when all was ready for going to sea. A half gale was blowing, and I thought of waiting over for another day, but the *Islander* was ready and impatient to take her first plunge into the Indian Ocean; so I up anchor, and she was off like a wild bird. The tide was against her, but running before the wind, she passed Booby Island, the outpost of Torres Strait, before sunset. When darkness came on, I took down the mainsail and slept, while my little ship drifted out on the Arafura sea.

For several days I sailed before a light east wind through green water where many sea snakes swam about, and each night the sun set in a red haze that was drifting out from Australia.

As the sun was setting on the tenth day out, I sighted Timor. For two days I coasted along this great island, which is high and mountainous throughout. As I approached the islands off the southwest end of Timor, night was coming on and a bank of dark clouds, driven before a gale, hid the land from view. In the darkness I stood offshore and hove to. The

Islander stood up to the storm well, but in this strange place, I was too uneasy to sleep. The wind blew its edge off before morning, and with daylight I made sail. Soon after, I sighted Rotti Island. I had no chart of the place, but I found my way through Semoa Strait and came up off Koepang, the port of Dutch Timor.

Attracted by a strange vessel in port, or possibly by the quarantine flag that I put out, a crowd collected on the beach, and some one called for me to come ashore. I rowed over to the beach, where the harbor-master, Mr. Smit, asked why I was flying the yellow flag. It seems that they do not use the quarantine flag in Dutch ports unless there is sickness on board. The crew of the *Islander* was healthy enough, and I wanted to show him the bill of health that I had paid ten shillings for at Thursday Island, but he did not care to see it. In the absence of the port doctor, he gave me permission to land and went to show me the town.

Koepang is a quaint little place, with a mixed population of Dutch officials, Chinese merchants, Malays, natives, and a few Arabs. The natives of Timor appear to be of the Papuan race. It was the dry season, and Timor had a barren appearance, but a small stream of water coming down from the hills is diverted into cement ditches and carried through the streets of the town, and the whitewashed houses of the Europeans were surrounded by green trees and flowers.

THE ISLANDER BEACHED FOR PAINTING ON PRINCE OF WALES ISLAND, TORRES STRAITS.

ANT HILL ON PRINCE OF WALES ISLAND.

LOOKING OFF SHORE FROM KOEPANG, DUTCH EAST INDIES.

FLYING-FISH COVE AND PHOSPHATE WORKS, CHRISTMAS ISLAND, INDIAN OCEAN.

There were very few people in the place who spoke English, but Mr. Smit took great pains in showing me about and explaining things. Selam, a commission merchant who changed my British shillings into Dutch gilders, conversed fluently. He was a political exile from Cashmere who had established himself in a house that some three hundred years ago had been the residence of the Portuguese governor, and a sign at his door made known the fact that he was an agent for Ford cars. We went for a ride in the first car that was brought to Timor. It was still a novelty, and one old woman whom we met seemed paralyzed with fright and stood staring in the middle of the road. When the driver honked his horn, she fell to the ground and scrambled out of the road on all fours.

Timor is a great island but still undeveloped. The only exports from Koepang were sandalwood, beeswax and hides. In the interior are great numbers of wild buffalo and deer. While I was in Koepang, a resident shot three deer on the edge of the town.

The most interesting place in Koepang was the public market where I went to buy fruits and vegetables. Here the different races gathered to display their strange wares and products. I was as strange to the people as they were to me, and as I walked about I could hear the word "American" passing on ahead. When I brought out my camera, a crowd collected and followed me about.

Among other articles from the market, I laid in a supply of sugar. The natives consume a large amount of sugar, which they make from a species of palm tree. When the palm puts forth its fruit stalk, the blossom buds are clipped off, and the sweet liquid that flows from the wounded stems is collected in pails made out of the palm leaf. The juice is drunk freely, both fresh and fermented, and one of the features of the market was to see the native girls vending the liquid from palm leaf pails and cups. When the juice is evaporated, it makes a sugar that much resembles maple sugar.

Rested and well supplied with fruits and vegetables, I sailed on the morning of August 28th, from Koepang for Christmas Island. The wind was fair out of Koepang Bay, but I drifted by the islands to the west almost becalmed; then I met the southeast trade wind and sailed away.

For several days the trades were light, and the *Islander* sailed leisurely on to the west, helped along by a westerly set of the current. It was at such times that I felt the monotony of being alone, but occasionally something of interest occurred to attract the attention.

One evening, at dusk, when the silence seemed almost painful, a whale rose to the surface and spouted close alongside the *Islander*. The deep, long-drawn-out sound of his breathing was startling and the proximity of this great creature gave me a feeling of awe. I contemplated what the consequences would be if one of them should collide with my ship. However, all of these animals, so far as I have observed, travel very leisurely when not alarmed, and it seems reasonable to suppose that they become aware of the presence of anything in their path in time to avoid coming in collision with it.

In these latitudes the phosphorescent sea sometimes takes on a very strange appearance at night. Once when the water was quite smooth, the whole expanse resembled a plain of snow, over which the *Islander* glided like a phantom ship.

But one morning the wind was blowing fresh and strong, and observations that day indicated that if I kept on sailing at the same rate, I should come up to Christmas Island in the night. In the evening the sky clouded up, and I was apprehensive lest I miss the island in the night. At sunset I hove to. At sunrise I stood off on the course, and soon after sighted the outlines of Christmas Island among the clouds ahead.

As I came into Flying Fish Cove I was surprised to see a steamship at the pier, decorated with bunting from stem to stern. A pilot came off and made my boat fast to a buoy and then invited me to come on board the *Islander,* for strangely enough, the name of the ship was the same as that of my little craft. The steamer belonged to the company that was working the phosphate deposits on the island, and a party was being given in honor of a departing employee. I had arrived just in time for dinner.

How strange it all seemed! All night, in loneliness and suspense, I had waited for the coming of day, and now I was seated at a banquet, and all about was the sound of happy voices. But if coming among a company like this on a little island in mid-ocean was strange to me, a lone man coming across the sea in a small boat was a surprise to them. One of the ladies present said to me, "Who are you anyway? You are not what you claim to be." She was thinking that I was a fictitious character, gotten up as part of the entertainment.

Christmas Island is a raised coral formation standing more than a thousand feet above the sea. It is covered with a dense forest, some of the trees being more than two hundred feet in height. Many land and sea birds make the island their home, and there are land crabs here with claws that will break open a coconut; but the commercial interest of the island is in the deposits of phosphate of lime. The whole island is under lease to the company operating the phosphate plant, and most of the European employees had their families with them, hence the merry party on board the steamer *Islander*.

I went with Superintendent McKinnon to inspect the phosphate plant. We ascended the steep cliff to the plateau on an incline cable railway. At the top of the incline we boarded a powered hand-car, and sped away in the delightfully cool air of the heights. A ride of about thirteen miles over a splendid railroad brought us to the phosphate quarry where busy Chinese workmen were clearing away the great forest trees, stripping off the surface soil, and excavating the phosphate. Mountain locomotives, "Made in Ohio," haul the phosphate across the plateau to where the cars are lowered down the cliff to the landing. The descending loaded cars raise the empty cars to the top of the cliff, and at the same time drive the dynamo that generates the electricity used about the plant.

Near the quarry I saw the abandoned camp of an English astronomical party that had left the island a short time before, after spending the greater part of a year making observations.

I spent five happy days with the people of the island and sailed well supplied through the generosity of the manager, George McMicken. I was busy on the last day, and the sun was setting when I made sail. My hosts, who gathered on the pier and watched the *Islander* glide away in the dusk, no doubt thought me strange indeed to sail at that hour.

During my stay at Christmas Island, Mr. Aliston, the wireless telegraph operator, had checked up the rate of my timepiece, and I felt the better for it when I set off to find the Cocos Islands. The run was uneventful except for a few rain squalls, and on fair days I had the company of many beautiful green Portuguese men-of-war drifting along with the trade wind. When I had finished plotting my position from observation of the sun at noon on the fifth day out, I began watching for the Cocos Islands. At half-past one o'clock coconut trees were showing above the sea, and all around myriads of birds were busy fishing.

Cocos Islands, where I arrived on September 15th, are scattered along a coral rim of horseshoe shape enclosing a lagoon about nine miles long, with an opening to the north. The land is nowhere more than twenty feet above the sea, but it is all planted to coconut trees that were visible from the deck of the *Islander* at a distance of about eight miles. Captain Land, of the steamship *Islander,* had given me a chart of the Cocos Islands, so I sailed into the lagoon and anchored close by the cable station on Direction Island and received a hearty welcome from the men of the Eastern Extension Telegraph Company, exiles, they call themselves.

Cocos is a far outlying station with a mail service four times in a year. It is an important station, and a large staff of operators are employed relaying the messages across the wide expanse of the Indian Ocean. When the *Islander* arrived they seemed to think they were having a run of visitors, as a short time previous a small craft, the *Shanghai,* in which three hardy adventurers were making a voyage from Shanghai to Denmark, had made them a call. They had thought the *Shanghai* a small boat with a small crew and were very much surprised when the *Islander* came in single-handed from America. They saw to it that I was well entertained and were interested in the story of my voyage, while I was no less interested in hearing them tell of experiences in some odd corners of the world. Several of them were interested in sailing, and the first thing that I noticed as I came in through the pass was the trim little sailing cutters gliding about the green lagoon.

The Keeling-Cocos Islands were taken possession

of by Captain J. Clunies Ross in 1827, and they are still owned by the Clunies Ross family, which own Christmas Island as well. Two members of the family reside on the islands with a colony of Malays to care for the coconut plantations that are the principal industry of the islands. At the invitation of Mr. J. S. Clunies Ross, the governor, I went over and spent the week-end with him on Home Island. Mr. Ross takes a great interest in designing and building the boats used about the islands for fishing and collecting the coconuts, as well as the little cutters that the cable men sail about the lagoon. Ever since the occupation of the islands, a boat building establishment has been maintained, and drawn up side by side under a roof were boats that each generation of the Rosses had built. In the days when the whaling industry was prosperous, many whalers put in at Cocos for repairs. Here Captain Slocum brought the *Spray* for cleaning and a coat of paint.

During the World War the German cruiser *Emden* sent a landing party ashore at Cocos to destroy the cable station, but not before the operators had communicated over their wireless set with the Australian warship *Sydney*. While the wreckers were busy at their task, the *Sydney* came up and drove the *Emden*, a battered wreck, onto the reef at North Keeling Island.

When the German landing party saw the fate that was overtaking their ship, they took possession of a small brig belonging to Ross and made their escape.

He recompensed himself by salvaging the valuable material from the wreck of the *Emden,* and when I visited the islands, the brass and bronze were being turned into boat fixtures in his shipyard.

I had no information other than the latitude and longitude of Rodriguez Island, my next calling place, but my friends at the cable station communicated with the station on Rodriguez and learned that the harbor was at Port Mathurin on the north side of the island. When I was ready to sail from the Keeling-Cocos Islands the *Islander* was a little deeper laden because of carrying gifts of the kind people there.

On the afternoon of September 23rd, I sailed on the long run down the Indian Ocean from Cocos Islands to Rodriguez. A good breeze was blowing as I cleared the islands and reefs; then a dark ominous cloud came rolling along from the southeast. The *Islander* drove off to the west before a gale, and I lost sight of the islands in the blinding rain.

For several days the weather was stormy with a rough sea, and I did not feel well. I had been living too well on shore. With only the jib and reefed mizzen sail set, the *Islander* sailed on day and night, while I stayed below out of the wet. Under this short sail, in one night, from sunset to sunrise, she made seventy miles; but I was being tossed about too much to sleep well.

It was on such days as these, after enjoying myself with friends on shore and then sailing into gloomy weather that I felt the solitude. But the first few days were the worst; then I began to look forward to my arrival at some new land and to speculate on what it would be like and whom I should meet there.

There was a week of stormy weather, and then the trade wind fell light and at times I was almost becalmed.

One day, when the *Islander* was moving along at a good clip before a fresh breeze, a school of small squid came on board from aft. They passed my head as if shot out of a gun, striking sails and rigging with such force as to knock off the heads of some.

They were evidently trying to escape an enemy that was pursuing them in the water, and took to the air in an effort to elude their pursuer. I was very much astonished, as I had never heard of squids taking to the air like flying fishes, and I do not think this fact is generally known. Later I observed many of them. They dart from the water with great speed, and as they leave the surface they eject a stream of water behind. They do not glide so far in the air as the flying fish, nor is their flight so well directed.

At last a blue peak stood out against the red and gold of the evening sky, and a welcome sight it was, for it marked the end of another long monotonous stretch of the voyage. I came up off the Island of Rodriguez early in the morning of October 13th, and while I was looking for a channel through the reef, a picturesque old pilot came out and directed me to an anchorage. Word of my coming had been received over the cable, and Magistrate Hanning came off with a boatload of visitors to welcome me to the island.

The *Islander* was anchored in a narrow channel through the reef, and there was not much swinging room. We had already put out two anchors, but the magistrate ordered the pilot to bring another anchor and line from the shore, saying, "We don't want the same thing to happen to the *Islander* that happened to the *Shanghai*."

It seems that the *Shanghai*, in whose wake I had been following from Cocos, had been anchored in this same place. She had swung with wind and tide till she went aground. With the falling tide she careened over so that an open port was under water and she filled, with bad results to her contents.

Rodriguez is a small mountainous island surrounded by reefs that in places extend more than four miles offshore. It supports a population of more than seven thousand inhabitants by fishing and agriculture, though I did not see a plow or an animal-drawn vehicle on the island. It is one of the happy isles where the people live in great simplicity. The cable station adds greatly to the importance of the place, and the members of the staff exerted themselves to make my stay pleasant. A small steamship from Mauritius calls five times a year with mail and carries away the produce of the island. This was a year of unusual events. In June there had arrived the Captain and seventeen men from the S.S. *Trevessa*, who had been twenty-three days at sea in an open boat, after their ship had foundered in the Indian Ocean west of Australia.

AMONG THE CAVES OF RODRIGUEZ ISLAND.

SCENE ON THE KEELING-COCOS ISLANDS, WHERE THE GERMAN RAIDER EMDEN WAS DESTROYED.

THE ISLANDER AT PORT LOUIS, MAURITIUS.

THE AUTHOR TAKES A ZULU TAXI AT DURBAN, SOUTH AFRICA.

Then the *Shanghai* with her adventurous crew had given them a call, and now the *Islander* had broken in on their round of placid days.

Aside from the picturesque scenery and its quaint people, the show place of Rodriguez is the caverns. The southwest end of the island is an upraised coral reef, and at some former period a stream from the hills had carved its way down through the reef to the sea. In this underground channel were scenes that reminded me of Doré's pictures. I first saw this cavern by the light of burning palm leaves. My guide carried a bundle of these under his arm, and lighted one after the other. I was concerned lest the palm leaves give out, but my guide had the same idea and made his exit in time.

Rodriguez was the only place where I had taken a pilot, and the good old man who brought me in through the reefs anchored the *Islander* to the cable. This I found out when I was making ready to leave. The pilot came out with his crew and tried to clear the anchors but only succeeded in getting more of the chain fouled in the mess below.

Along with the pilot had come Thomas, one of his friends, presumably to act as interpreter, as the old man only spoke patois. While we were busy forward, Thomas went in to investigate the cabin. Chancing to go below, I missed a sum of money that I had laid on the table to pay the pilot with. Thomas, who was watching me from the companionway, said, "What are you looking for, your money? I have it here in my pocket." Saying at the same time, that he had taken it to keep one of the black men from getting it.

Along in the evening the pilot gave it up as a bad job, took his crew and went ashore. Thomas went with them, taking the money. I said nothing; he was the pilot's friend, and if he kept it, the old man would not get it.

The next day I discovered that my photographs were missing. This was more serious than the loss of a few shillings, so I started at once to find Thomas. Thomas was a Mauritian who spoke English, and apparently a man of some education. I found him on his bed looking rather feverish and a colored boy applying wet cloths to his head. He produced the money but said he had never seen the photographs and knew nothing about them, and he was so earnest about it that I concluded that he had not taken them. On making further inquiry, I was told that Thomas was subject to mental derangement, and that most likely he did have them. The magistrate got word of it and wanted to send a policeman to get them, but I thought best to try a more tactful method. I went to Thomas again and asked him to help me find the photographs. The idea seemed to please him very much and he said he would do it. He said he knew who took them and could lay his hand on him at any time. But his head ached and he would have to wait till the sun went down before he could go out to look for them. In the end he said, "Your photographs are not stolen, I have them. I took you for a German."

He brought out the photographs and then demonstrated his affection for me with a kiss.

There were no Tuamotuan divers in Rodriguez, so I left two anchors hooked to the cable. In the early morning of October 28th, I sawed off the anchor chains and made sail.

Before the gentlest of winds I sailed from Rodriguez. On the second day out I crossed a meridian halfway around the world from my home port. After four days of light weather, the wind breezed up and blew hard with rain, sending the *Islander* flying down to Mauritius.

The people of Mauritius took a great interest in my voyage, and scarcely a day passed without some one showing me some special kindness. Mauritius is a beautiful place and I had many opportunities of seeing it. Friends came with motor cars to show me about, and I was given a pass over the Mauritius Railway.

Mauritius has a very large Indian population, and I was surprised at the number of these people who came on board. Some of them appeared to believe I was a sort of holy man. A number of Bombay boatmen were constantly employed around the waterfront carrying passengers to and from the vessels anchored in the harbor, and I earned their good will when I permitted them to bring on board any one who wished to come. I had been told that I would have to keep a watch or everything loose would be stolen, but I always treated these strange people as guests, and I never had cause to suspect them of taking anything.

One day a party of Mohammedan graybeards came to interview me. The three wise men of the East interested me quite as much as I did them. With all possible dignity I handed them down the companion-way and when all were seated, brought out my charts and souvenirs of other lands. They pored over these gravely, and through their interpreter asked many learned questions about my voyage. They seemed well pleased with what they saw and heard, and I believe they were convinced that I had crossed the waters alone. Surely my fame was spreading.

I met Mr. Vincent Smart of the Mauritius Public Works Department while he was on a visit to Rodriguez. At the time I was engaged in a futile effort to get my anchors clear of the telegraph cable. Having in mind the lost anchors, Mr. Smart and Lieutenant Goodwin made arrangements to have me tell about my travels before an audience of soldiers and civilians in the Barracks Hall, at Vacoa. I sailed the voyage over again with less stormy weather than I anticipated, and at the close of the talk I met several prominent people who were quite content to do the cruise in this way. The proceeds of the entertainment paid for the lost anchors several times over.

As a finale to the many acts of kindness shown the *Islander,* Taylor, Smith & Company took her up on their marine railway and gave her a coat of paint.

I spent a month amid pleasant surroundings and would have lingered, but with the coming in of December the people began to talk of hurricanes, and it was time for the *Islander* to sail again.

On the fourth of December the *Islander* well fitted in every way sailed from Port Louis for South Africa. A party of friends came on board to sail with me out of the harbor, while the waterfront was black with the crowd that gathered to see us off. At the outer buoy my friends boarded their launch, gave three cheers and turned back, while I, once more alone on the *Islander,* sailed out into a rain storm that swept down the shore of the island. When night came on, the wind fell light, and Mauritius was still in sight at the end of the second day. It was the third day when I drifted by Reunion Island, a remarkable body of land that rises above the Indian Ocean to a height of more than ten thousand feet. I longed to go on shore, but the season of hurricanes bade me hurry from these latitudes.

A strong wind sprang up and I rapidly left the deeply scarred mountains of Reunion behind. With the rising wind I began reefing the sails when I was struck squarely on top of the head by the main boom and finished the job with blood streaming down in my eyes. In a few days the southeast trade wind, that had carried me so far across the Pacific and Indian oceans, died down, and as I approached Madagascar a storm blew up from the south.

The next day as I sailed by a vast black cloud that hung over the island, I caught a momentary glimpse of a conical peak through a rift. On the second day the cloud lifted and I saw land close at hand. A little later I made out that I was passing Cape St. Mary. It was noon on December 15th when the *Islander* shaped a course from the Cape. With the clearing weather the mainsail was spread to the fresh breeze and at sunset she had made forty-two miles. For the most part the winds in the Mozambique Channel were light, but a week later I had my first sight of Africa. As I approached the coast a gale came down out of the northeast, and all night the *Islander* lay hove to, plunging into a rough sea. With the noise of the wind, the violent motion, and the excitement of being close in with the land I got no sleep. Through the night I watched a fire that was burning on the hills, and by it knew that I was not drifting south with the current.

With the dawn, the beautiful green hills of Natal lay close at hand, and my first impression of Africa was good. The gale was dying out and the last of the northeast wind brought me into the harbor at Durban. The *Islander* was met just inside the entrance by Pilot Watkins, who was on the lookout for my arrival and came with a launch and towed her up to a berth in the creek, where she had three steam whalers for company.

XII

Africa

I SHALL always retain many pleasant memories
of the days that I spent at Durban. I arrived on
December 23rd, in good time for an invitation to a
Christmas dinner. Such was the hospitality of the
place that my little galley fell into disuse, as I dined
out most every day, and the whalers alongside seemed
to consider it a slight if I did not join them at their
mess.

At no place was greater interest taken in my voyage.
As the *Islander* was alongside the dock with a gang-
plank out, a continual stream of visitors came on
board. Nor did they all come to see only. At least
twenty made application for a berth on the *Islander*.
The idea of seeing the world from the deck of a small
vessel appeals to many. A young man of Johannes-
burg, who applied by letter, did not wait for an answer
but came the next day to press his application in person.

At nearly every port where I called, some one had
taken it on himself to look after my interests. Here
a number of new friends exerted themselves to make
my stay pleasant, and one of these, Mr. Andrew
Goldie, on learning that I had a lantern and slides,

made arrangements for the residents of several communities in and around Durban to hear about my voyage and the countries that I had visited. The Point Yacht Club also gave an entertainment for my benefit. The proceeds of these entertainments went a long way toward making the latter end of my voyage a success.

In the meanwhile I put in new and stronger standing rigging on the *Islander,* bent on her best suit of sails and made ready for the passage around the Cape of Good Hope. I had intended sailing early in February, but my lecture program lengthened out, and I was still at Durban telling the people about my voyage when the worst southeaster in years swept the Cape. When it was over I put to sea.

On February 27, 1924, I put to sea alone after turning down several tempting offers from parties who wished to join my ship as mate. My good friend, Captain Watkins, came to help me get under way and then sailed the *Islander* down to the jetties. When I was clear of the land, the wind fell light but the Agulhas Current carried my little bark steadily away to the south.

I met with much head wind and at times there was little wind at all. For two days the *Islander* lay hove to under reefed mizzen sail and storm jib in a westerly gale on the Agulhas Bank, with the big seas driving her back along her course. It was the wildest looking sea that I had encountered in the *Islander,* and often the big combers would throw her bow off and slue her around almost beam on. The storm jib split open, so I took it in and put out the sea anchor but it did not work well. It appeared to be too light to sink to the proper depth and was not large enough. I began to repair the jib and found it an awful task to sew the stiff, wet canvas, while the *Islander* was trying to stand on end. I broke several needles but got the job done after a fashion. All this time I imagined that I was drifting nearer the land, and it looked close. With some exertion I hauled in the sea anchor and set the jib, after which the *Islander* began to draw slowly out from the shore, and I was content to go below out of the wet till the gale blew itself out. During another westerly gale I lay under the shelter of Cape Infanta for two days.

During my passage around the Cape, first the east wind and then the west wind surged around the great headland in periods of two or three days each. And so they blew all the while I was in South Africa. Much of the time these winds are light, but often enough they are blowing a gale; then in its turn the west wind batters the Cape with mighty rollers that have been gathering momentum all the way from Cape Horn. All the time I was sailing along in sight of the great sand dunes of the African shore and right in the track of the steamers passing around the Cape of Good Hope. The proximity of these two menaces to single-handed navigation caused some apprehension whenever I tried to sleep.

I sailed from Cape Infanta as the west wind was

dying down. The swell was still running high, and the wind fell so light off the point that I had an anxious hour getting clear of the rocky headland. The east wind breezed up during the night, and at sunrise I was close up to Cape Agulhas, the southern extremity of Africa. The wind came stronger during the day, and I glided quickly by dark crags that were very different from the green hills of Natal. At sunset a gale was blowing, and while the *Islander* raced on before it, I watched for the light on the Cape of Good Hope that soon after flashed up on our course. Before midnight I had rounded the bold rocky headland and gladly headed away to the northward and into the Atlantic Ocean.

When I came up under the shelter of the land, I let the *Islander* run on under easy sail while I went below and turned in, for I was wet, cold, and tired. When I came out in the morning, my vessel was becalmed in the lee of Table Mountain. Here I drifted most of the day before getting into Cape Town; but I was content, for behind lay the stormy cape and before me lay the grandest sight the whole world around.

Wafted along by the faint breezes that occasionally stirred the region under the great cliffs, late in the afternoon, the *Islander* came up with a line of whitecaps and the strong east wind sweeping round the north side of Table Mountain struck right in our teeth. With sheets close-hauled and the spray flying we beat up to Green Point, where we were met by Pilot Short in a launch and towed to a snug berth in the docks. After eighteen days of almost constant looking out for steamers, breakers, and changes of wind, I was quite ready for a rest in the quiet of the harbor.

Among the first of many visitors to come on board at Cape Town were Commodore Warington Smyth and members of the Royal Cape Yacht Club, and I have many pleasant memories of my association with these hearty good fellows who find sport in spreading their canvas to the bracing breezes off the Cape.

I have never seen a city with a grander setting than Cape Town, and the climate, which is much the same as that of California, was much appreciated after my two years in the tropics. While I rested from the sea, I had many interesting excursions around the wonderful Cape Peninsula and Table Mountain. The greater part of African trees and plants were new to me, and few countries surpass South Africa in the variety and beauty of its wild flowers.

After I had had a few days' rest from the sea, one of my yachting friends, Mr. Burton Tubb, arranged for a cruise to some small islands off the coast that were the breeding place of innumerable sea birds.

Mr. Tubb was a very keen sailing man, so I gave him an opportunity to see what he could do with the *Islander,* but on the run to Saldanha Bay there was a surprise coming to him. When night came we shortened sail a bit, lashed the tiller and went below to have a hot dinner and then turned into our berths for a few hours' sleep. As there were no lights of any descrip-

tion around the entrance to Saldanha Bay it was necessary to keep a good course if we were to find it in
the night. Consequently Mr. Tubb went frequently
on deck to look at the compass and expressed himself
as amazed to find the boat running steadily on before
the wind. Before our distance was run down we put
on more sail and stood by. At last there was a sound
of heavy surf, and we found ourselves right in the
fairway to the bay. We ran into quiet water, rounded
to and let go the anchor. With the coming of daylight
I saw we were in a beautiful landlocked bay about ten
miles long; the finest natural harbor in South Africa.

One on either hand at the entrance to Saldanha Bay
are two small rocky islands around which the mighty
Atlantic swells surge and foam. These islands are
government reservations, and a keeper, with a crew
of men, is stationed on each to collect the guano deposited by the myriads of birds that make them their
homes.

We sailed down to Malegassen Island and anchored
in the best lee we could find. Going ashore in my
small dinghy was a bit of adventure in itself. Watching our opportunity, we dashed in on a swell and
landed on a flat rock, where the men of the island
stood waiting to grab the dinghy as soon as it touched.

The Island was thickly populated with gannets,
locally called Malegassen birds, that showed no more
fear of man than so many barnyard fowls, though
they had a disposition to use their spearlike beaks
when pressed too closely. We spent some interesting

hours getting acquainted with the birds, then sailed across to Jutten Island where we found a better lee and anchored for the night. The next morning we started out to explore the island.

Jutten Island is a reservation for cormorants but there were many penguins also. The cormorants are more valuable birds for the guano deposited, and, as they are shy birds, they were protected from the more aggressive penguins by a stone fence around their roosting ground in the center of the island. The penguins, not being able to fly and not being very good on foot, had to content themselves outside the fence.

On the windward side of the island there were picturesque rocks on which the westerly swell was expending its force in masses of foam. Here, the keeper informed us, gold coins are occasionally washed up during heavy storms. It appears that when the British took the Cape from the Dutch, a Dutch ship that was being pursued was set on fire and sunk in a small bay on the windward side. This was getting interesting, but all thought on our part of taking part in a treasure hunt was cut short by the wind's suddenly shifting to the north. Taking along a crate of penguin eggs that the keeper of the island gave us, we hurried on board to get up sail and claw off a lee shore.

We came up off Dassen Island late in the evening. A squall was approaching and the sky looked very black to windward. The wind was now northeast so it was not safe to enter the little harbor on the north end of the island. We ran in close on the east side and anchored in the best place we could find. The mizzen sail was left set and the jib ready to break out, for if the chain parted we would have to make sail in a hurry. It was now raining and blowing hard, so we dived below, built a roaring fire, and were soon eating fried penguin eggs and hot cakes. We kept a close watch until midnight, when the wind came round to northwest and we joyfully turned in. The next morning the wind was southeast, and we found a more comfortable berth in the little bay at the north end.

Dassen Island is the place to see penguins. There is much sandy ground where the birds dig out depressions for their nests, some of them burrowing underground. The comical looking birds came trooping ashore by the thousands like so many soldiers, and showing a disposition to contest the ground with invading men. One that I picked up bit my hand savagely, and my friend Tubb, who broke through into an underground burrow, scrambled out with the occupant clinging to his leg. The birds had reason to be in a bad humor, for about a dozen men were employed on the island gathering their eggs for the Cape Town market, where they bring a higher price than the ordinary barnyard product.

Interesting as the birds were, there was another scene that attracted my attention with a strange fascination. It was the welter of broken water that extends for almost two miles out from the west side of the island. Out there the great swells that have been gathering momentum all the way from Cape Horn crash and tumble over a maze of rocks and reefs. While I looked on the scene, I wondered what chance a castaway would have getting ashore through the turmoil. I remembered this later when I had a narrow escape on the rocky coast a few miles away. I don't know if the scene impressed Mr. Tubb, as it was his home coast, but he suddenly concluded to return to his wife and babies in Cape Town, and we sailed out of the cove on Dassen Island.

On the course to Cape Town the southeast wind was right in our teeth, but that seemed to suit my sailing companion just as well as a fair wind. It was oilskin weather, and at dusk we tied in two reefs. Mr. Tubb was so enthusiastic about sailing that he seemed to be content to stay at the tiller all night if supplied with an occasional cup of hot tea. Toward morning I relieved him, so that he might get warmed up and have a bit of sleep, but in a couple of hours he was at it again. We came up to Robbin Island at dawn, and as it was Mr. Tubb's birthplace, we had intended calling, but by this time the southeaster was churning up such a sea that it was not safe to land, so we beat on through it to Cape Town. Mr. Tubb afterwards confided to me that he had hoped that we would have met up with a real storm, so that he might see how the *Islander* would act when hove to. His ideas were very different from mine. I always wish for fair winds and make the best of what comes.

We returned from our outing with the birds in time to join the fleet of the Royal Cape Yacht Club for their annual opening cruise around Table Bay. The *Islander* was not sailed single-handed that day. Commodore Smyth sent two sailor lads from his *Irex* for her crew, and Billie Watson, the honorable handicapper of the club, came along to get her rating. I think one can appreciate company better after a period of solitude, and, if the *Islander* enjoyed the day as I did, we had a glorious time. The *Islander* was not in the best of sailing trim, for her bottom was a veritable marine garden, and she was trailing along a wonderful collection of weeds and moss. I believe every boat in the fleet sailed around her that day, but when the formation went gliding by the pleasure pier, where the spectators had gathered to view the parade, no yacht came in for more attention. Some weeks later, after she had been hauled out on the slip and given a new coat of bottom paint, they learned that she was not the slowest boat ever.

A pleasant incident of my stay at the Cape was a visit to the famous Cape Observatory. I met Dr. Spencer-Jones, royal astronomer, at the Owl Club, and as he had conducted an astronomical expedition to Christmas Island, we found it interesting to compare notes. At his invitation, I called on him at the Observatory, where I was shown the various instruments, and the method of regulating the Observatory clock by the stars was explained to me. It was certainly more accurate than my method of finding the time at sea, and wonderfully interesting to a navigator.

At the suggestion of my friends of the Yacht Club, I told about my adventures to an audience at the Railway Institute. For the occasion I made up a new set of slides with which to illustrate my talk. The yachtsmen and their friends were a very appreciative audience, and my effort to entertain them attracted the attention of some of the Cape educators. I was invited to appear before the students of the Rondebosch Boys' High School, and then addressed a crowded house at the South African College. According to the reports in the local newspapers, I became something of a hero among the boys of these institutions. A little later the members of the Mountain Club called on me to tell them all about it. I got on famously with the mountain climbers, for I had been a mountaineer long before I became a sailor. Aside from the pleasure it gave me to meet with so many warm hearts, the financial results enabled me to carry on without having to cable home for funds.

The newspaper accounts of my voyage called the attention of several adventurous persons to the possibility of cruising about the world in a small yacht, and I received as many applications for the position of mate on the *Islander* at Cape Town as I had at Durban. But after rounding the stormy Cape alone, I was determined to bring my vessel home singlehanded.

While the usual preparation for going to sea was under way, the Royal Cape Yacht Club, to make sure that I did not arrive at my next port hungry, placed an order with a firm of ship chandlers to put on board supplies to the amount of ten pounds sterling.

On June 3, 1924, the northwest gale that had been blowing died down, and I sailed for the Island of St. Helena. The pilot launch *Eveline* towed the *Islander* out of the docks to where a scant breeze gave steerage-way. A steam tug came out at the same time towing a bark that almost rolled her lower yards into the water when she met the heavy westerly swell. And rolling still, the tug towed her straight out to sea until she was lost to sight. The sky was gray and wintry with a thin drizzle of rain.

The expected southeast wind came up light, and for two days I drifted slowly north along the coast, too close in to sleep with any feeling of security. On the third night out, when I was a little farther offshore, I went below to get some rest. I slept, and awoke when the *Islander* took to the ground.

I sprang up to find that I was in the breakers. At first I saw only a turmoil of white water, and each swell was pushing my boat farther into it. My first thought was that I had struck on a reef and that we were going to pass on over it. But I soon saw the beach and then made out the line of the sand hills against the cloudy sky. When I saw that we were stranded sure enough, I said, "My voyage ends right here." At that moment I had little idea that I would ever get her off again, and as I stood in the companion-way, a spectator of what was taking place, I was already picturing myself walking home.

THE LIGHTHOUSE ON THE CAPE OF GOOD HOPE.

THE OPENING CRUISE OF THE ROYAL CAPE YACHT CLUB,
CAPETOWN, SOUTH AFRICA.

PENGUINS ON DASSEN ISLAND, SOUTH AFRICA.

THE ISLANDER ASHORE IN NORTHWEST BAY, CAPE PROVINCE,
SOUTH AFRICA.

It did not take the surf long to throw the *Islander* up on the beach, where she lay on her beam ends with an occasional sea breaking over her. I now began to take stock. It was about two o'clock in the morning, and a glance at the compass showed that the wind was coming out of the northwest. The wind had changed while I slept, and the *Islander* had turned and sailed in onto the shore. I took in the sails, then turned into the berth that was on the lower side and tried to sleep once more.

When daylight came, I saw that I was in a small bay, with a sand beach at the head and rocks on either side. The *Islander* had chosen her resting place well. The tide was out, and I could walk all around her. A ragged ledge of rocks, uncovered at low water, over which she had passed, accounted for the after part of the keel and the rudder being battered and chewed up to some extent as well as the loss of the rotator of the log.

I crossed over the sand hills, and about half a mile away came to some buildings, the home of Farmer Pienaar, on whose estate I had been cast away. Here I learned that I was stranded in Northwest Bay, some fifteen miles north of Saldanha Bay. The farmer's son, Attie Pienaar, volunteered to take his motorcycle and go with me to see if we could find assistance.

At Vredenburg, some seven miles inland, we met a brother of Secretary Wilman, of the Royal Cape Yacht Club. Mr. Wilman introduced me to Mr. Cassell, who happened to be in town that day. Mr. Cassell was manager for H. J. C. Stephan, who had large farming and fishing interests in the district. Almost the first words he said to me were, "When the weather gets so that we can, we will come and take you off." Taking his car, he came out to the Pienaar farm to see the stranded vessel and look over the situation. The prospect of sailing home in the *Islander* was brighter.

When the *Islander* sailed herself ashore, the sea was comparatively smooth, but all day the wind had been increasing, and by night a northwest gale was blowing. The white-crested billows came rolling into the bay and broke in masses of foam around the stranded boat. But I was tired enough to sleep. Toward morning, when the tide was high, I was turned out of my berth when a large wave broke over the *Islander* and the backwash from it threw her over and down hill on the other beam ends with great violence. There was a crash of glass and other breakables, and I heard her timbers creak. The incoming sea lifted her into her first position and then the backwash threw her downhill again. Again and again she was thrown from beam ends to beam ends. She was built strong, but I knew she was not going to stand this long. I put on the sails and flattened in the sheets, but an occasional big sea would still throw her over against the pressure of the wind. I then cut loose the lift from the main boom and bent another line to it. This gave me a line from the fore masthead. Between seas I carried this ashore, and with it the violent motion was stopped.

In the gray dawn a wild scene presented itself. The

angry sea washed the bedraggled *Islander* heavily, while masses of wind-driven foam flew over and around her. I never saw such a place for foam which was drifted knee-deep in the brush on shore. The storm had driven the *Islander* a little higher on the beach, and as the tide went out, sand formed around her until she was firmly embedded. During the day the wind moderated, and I settled down to await events with what patience I could.

The *Islander* was not the first vessel to get into trouble in the bay, and one had not been so fortunate. Near where she lay was the grave of the engineer of a Portuguese steamer, who had been drowned when his ship had run ashore in a fog.

But for the near-by farm the place would have been desolate enough. The kind-hearted Pienaars insisted on my coming to eat with them, saying that I could not cook on my boat when it was lying on its side. If I did not go to the farmhouse at mealtime, they sent some one to the boat with lunch and a pail of milk. They wanted me to come to the farmhouse to sleep, but I would not leave my boat overnight, and then I had arranged the berth on the lower side so that it was quite comfortable. Unlike some stranded vessels, my boat was not filled with water. When I went to the farm on Saturday, I met the youngest member of the family, Aletta Pienaar, who had been away at school when I was cast up from the sea. I had to tell her all about my voyage. She brought out her school atlas and questioned me carefully about where

I had been and where I intended going, marking down my route, so that she might be able to tell her schoolmates about it. Mrs. Pienaar, who was listening to our talk, said to me, "How is it that when you are sailing west all of the time, you are going to get back to your home again?" The bright young scholar said, "Oh, mother, the world is round."

The weather cleared the next day to the extent that many people from up country came to see the boat that had sailed ashore. A reporter for a Cape Town daily motored up from the city, and altogether I had a busy day recounting my experience. Every one seemed to think that I had had a marvelous escape when the *Islander* found her way into this bay. I was told that from Saldanha Bay to Paternoster, a distance of twenty-five miles, the coast was all rocks except Northwest Bay, and even here there is a rock ledge in the entrance. At any other place on that stretch of coast I should have been lucky to have gotten on shore alive, let alone saving my boat. Mr. Cassell came also, bringing along Captain Zamudis, of the steamer *Luna,* and Mr. Schwirner, both from Stephan's lobster cannery some miles up the coast. They were to superintend the work of getting the *Islander* afloat once more, but the surf was still too strong and nothing could be done until it went down.

For a few days more I kept watch by the sand dunes, where Farmer Pienaar's sheep and ostriches roamed. Then one morning the *Luna* came into the bay. Captain Zamudis and a boat crew landed bringing planks, rollers, and gear. Mr. Schwirner and a party of men came overland by automobile. The sand was dug away and the *Islander* raised with jacks until the planks and rollers could be placed underneath.

The second launching of the *Islander* attracted more attention than did her first, and many people came from the countryside, including women and children. The Pienaars brought coffee and lunch for all, and altogether it was quite a merry affair.

It was no easy task to move the *Islander,* and it was the evening of the second day when she was brought down to the water at low tide. The *Luna* had anchored and let out a good length of chain. The end of a heavy line was landed from her and made fast to the *Islander.* Heaving in on the anchor chain of the *Luna* put a heavy strain on the line. This brought the *Islander's* head around to the sea, but there she lay with the seas bashing her from side to side. It was more exciting for me than the stranding had been. The spectators built fires on shore and waited to see what would happen. I was stationed on board with a lantern to signal the *Luna* if all was holding together. It was high tide at eleven o'clock that night and it was not until then that the *Islander* began to move out. She thumped along on the bottom for a distance and then went off into deeper water. "Hurrah for the *Islander,* how gladly she rose to the swells." After eight days on the beach she was back in her element once more.

The *Luna* moved out into deeper water and anchored with the *Islander* swinging astern. I expected to find her leaking, but I found less than ten gallons of water in the pump well, and that had washed down the companionway on the night of the storm. When it was bailed out, no more came in. She was not leaking a drop.

The weather did not look so good the next morning, and at daybreak Captain Zamudis left for Paternoster Bay, without landing for his gear or my dinghy. As the *Luna,* towing the *Islander* astern, steamed along the rocky coast, I had an opportunity of seeing how fortunate I had been when I was cast up in Northwest Bay. So far as I could see, the whole shore was buttressed with granite rocks. A line of these giant rocks, jutting out from a point of land at the entrance of Paternoster Bay, forms a shelter behind which is located one of Mr. Stephan's fisheries.

When we arrived in Paternoster Bay, the anchors, chains, and stores that had been taken on board the *Luna,* were stowed on the *Islander* once more, and she was made ready to sail again. Later in the day, my dinghy arrived. It came overland on a four-horse wagon, that had been sent to recover the gear left on the beach by the *Luna.* Seven pounds also arrived, sent from Cape Town by friends, who thought I might need some money. But there seemed to be no opportunity for me to use money in this part of the country. It seemed best for me to repair the *Islander* at Cape Town. Before I sailed the next day, Mr. Cassell gave me a piece of Australian jarra wood with which to make her a new shoe. I arrived at Cape Town on June 17th, having light winds all the way.

The first thing that I did was to call on Mr. Stephan and thank him for what he had done. He wanted to know what else he could do for me. I told him that he had done enough. My boat was afloat once more, and I could shift for myself.

The *Islander* was hauled out on the marine ways, and I went to work getting her in shape once more. The after part of the shoe was torn away until the rudder pintle was gone, and the side of the keel and the rudder were scarred where they had come in contact with a rock. A few splinters had been raised on the bilge, but no serious damage had been done. Many people came to see her, and almost every one expressed the opinion that I was lucky to get her off the beach, and that she came off with so little damage was a wonder.

I cut away the damaged wood and spiked on the new shoe. The splinters were planed off the keel and bilge, and a new coat of paint applied. Three days' work put her in as good condition as ever, and her cargo had not been damaged in the least.

I don't suppose any one who was ever stranded on a strange shore got off so fortunately. I was no worse off in a material way, and I was a great deal richer in experience. It was certainly humiliating to have my boat cast up on the beach through my own carelessness, but I felt repaid for all the hardship just to meet the generous people who came to my assistance. Now that

I had returned to the Cape, I remembered that when I had sailed it seemed as if I were leaving in too much of a hurry, and I was glad to be back once more.

It was now winter at the Cape and northwest gales were frequent, so I decided that it would be more profitable to remain in pleasant surroundings than to be contending with stormy weather. My many friends were glad to see me back and saw to it that I was not lonesome. Some of them wanted me to locate at the Cape. The time passed quickly and with September I was making ready to sail once more, and when the *Islander* put to sea she was in better condition and better supplied than when she left her home port.

XIII

Atlantic Ocean

ON September 22nd, for the second time, I sailed from Cape Town for the Island of St. Helena. A southeast wind was blowing and held on. At nightfall I was nearing the place where I met disaster before. I laid a course to the northwest and kept watch all through the night. When morning came only a haze in the horizon indicated where Africa lay. On the second night I was tired with my long watch and turned in to sleep, having no fear of going ashore before I should awake.

It was springtime at the Cape when I left, and I expected to run right into warmer weather, but instead it was cold and gloomy. The wind continued fair and I ran into the southeast trade winds, but never had I seen so much cloudy weather in the trades. I seldom had an unobscured sight of the sun, and I had lost the rotator of the log when the *Islander* ran ashore in Northwest Bay, so my dead reckoning was rather hazy. I began to fear that I should miss the island. On the fifth day out I sighted a Union Castle boat on the way to the Cape, so I was not far out in my reckoning, and I followed a course calculated to bring me up to the latitude of the island well to the eastward.

Much of the time the wind was blowing strong, and I found that the sails were getting rotten. First the jib split. That was mended and then the cringle in the clew of the mainsail tore out and the sail was torn. I let the yawl run on under the jib and mizzen sail, and that night the jib split again. It's not so nice on a rough night to crawl out on the bowsprit and change the jib when you are going to get ducked in the sea while doing it, and there is no one around to pick you up if you fall off. But it had to be done, and the next day the wet sails had to be mended.

Flying fish are usually numerous where the trade winds blow, but I was near to the latitude of St. Helena before one appeared. It departed from the water close alongside, and I saw that it had wings shaped like those of a butterfly. It was the first butterfly flying fish that I had seen.

On the seventeenth day out I had a fair observation of the sun and calculated my position to be about sixty miles east of St. Helena. When night came on I hove to. I was not sure of my longitude, and I had noticed an absence of the sea birds that usually indicate the proximity of land. Morning dawned with clouds and gloom; I had not been under way half an hour when the clouds opened in the west and right ahead I saw the outlines of the cliffs of St. Helena.

From the sea St. Helena has a barren, desolate appearance, like a gigantic cinder afloat in mid-ocean. I can imagine how grim those cliffs looked to Napoleon when, from the deck of the *Northumberland*, he saw them for the first time.

It was noon before I came up off Jamestown. Harbormaster Pink directed me to a mooring in the roadstand to which the *Islander* was securely fastened, which was the extent of the formalities connected with my arrival at the island. A heavy swell was breaking on the shore and the landing did not look too good, but a boatman, who came to look over the *Islander,* gave me instructions about landing. The trade winds blow almost continuously at St. Helena, and, although the roadstead at Jamestown is in the lee, a swell comes round the ends of the island. There is a continual surge of the sea around the end of the wharf, but watching for a favorable opportunity I ran in, jumped out on the landing steps, and hauled the dinghy up on the landing out of the way of the sea. All quite easy. At times, when there is a storm in the South Atlantic, heavy rollers break on the shore. Sometimes it was exciting, but there was no time during my stay at the island when I could not land with the dinghy on the wharf.

St. Helena has some good roads, but there are no motor vehicles using them. A motorcycle was once brought to the island, but it was not allowed to be taken off the wharf. For this reason walking was a pleasure, and as there were many places of interest to be seen, I spent much of my time rambling about the place. As one climbs out of the narrow valley from Jamestown, the scanty cactus and aloes that cling to the red-brown cliffs give way to a more luxuriant vegetation. Up in the highlands, where the trade winds give out their moisture, there are rural scenes as beautiful as are to be found in any country. Here trees from different climes grow side by side, and the Norfolk Island pine rises above the yellow blossoms of the English gorse.

In the days when the commerce of the world was carried on in sailing ships, St. Helena lay right in the track of the homeward bound East Indiamen, and there they called for water and a supply of meat, fruit, and vegetables. Then it was a prosperous place, but steamships and the Suez Canal have left it only an island of romance. Many of its inhabitants have had to seek employment elsewhere. Flax is grown on the damp highlands and is the principal export of the place. There is a lace school, and very fine lace is made on the island, but many of the families depend on the workers who go out to other lands and send their earnings home.

Perhaps it was because of their isolation that the people took so much interest in the little vessel calling their way. Arrangements were made to have me tell about my voyage and show the pictures I had made of other lands. The hall was crowded but still there were some who did not get in to hear it, so I had to tell it all over once more.

In 1898, when Captain Joshua Slocum was circumnavigating the world in the *Spray*, he called at St. Helena, and Mr. R. A. Clark, an American residing

THE ISLANDER LYING OFF ST. HELENA.

PLANTATION HOUSE, THE GOVERNOR'S RESIDENCE, ST. HELENA.

THE DEW POND ON THE SUMMIT OF GREEN MOUNTAIN, ASCEN-
SION ISLAND.

MAN-O'-WAR BIRDS ON BOATSWAIN-BIRD ROCK, ASCENSION
ISLAND.

there, gave him a goat. Not having the heart to kill and eat it, he put it ashore at Ascension Island after it had eaten his chart of the West Indies and his last hat. Mr. Clark was still living at St. Helena and related to me many incidents of his long residence on the island, as well as the story of the goat he gave to Captain Slocum, but I was not taking any live stock on board the *Islander*.

On the afternoon of November 22nd I was ready for sea once more. Mr. Clark came to see me away, saying it was the second time he had seen a single-handed circumnavigator off from the island. He sailed out a little way with me and then turned back with a boatman. When the sun had set I was far out from St. Helena.

The run to Ascension Island was one of the easiest of the voyage. Before a light trade wind and over a smooth sea the *Islander* glided along, requiring little attention day or night. As she rippled her way through the dark blue sea, startled flying fishes darted from underneath her bow and sailed away to right and left. Occasionally I saw the spout of a whale. Now and then a tropic bird came out of the blue sky and circled around the little vessel. Sailing ships seem to be a novelty to the sea birds in this part of the ocean nowadays.

As the sun was setting on November 30th, I sighted the peak of Ascension Island on the horizon. I lowered all sail but the jib and drifted on through the night. At three o'clock I put on sail and came up to the island at sunrise. A sail in the roadstead was not long in attracting attention. Mr. Drew, the harbor-master, came off and the *Islander* was securely fastened to a mooring where she would ride safely when the rollers came in. A party from the cable station came off to pay their respects and gave me to understand that if I wanted anything to let them know about it. At the time of my visit the only residents on the island were the people connected with the Eastern Telegraph Company and the Ascension Island Guano Company, but I could not have been better received anywhere.

Ascension Island was very interesting to me as it was the best opportunity I had had to see what a volcanic island was like. From the anchorage the island appears to be a lava bed above which rise numerous cinder cones. It is a desert except for the highest peak, Green Mountain, which pierces the trade wind clouds and gets enough rain to support a growth of vegetation. Its raw appearance has given rise to the assertion that it is one of the newest islands in the world, and that Great Britain had possession of it before it was cold. But it is probable that the volcanic fires died out ages ago and parts of the island, including Green Mountain, appear to be very ancient. There are reasons for placing St. Helena and Ascension among the oldest lands now existing on the surface of the globe.

Myriads of sea birds make the island their breeding place. It was the season for wide-awakes when I arrived, and they were the source of the egg supply of the place. In company with a party of residents I went to see a place called the Wide-awake Fair. A walk of about two miles across the sun-baked waste brought us to a sandy plain where millions of wide-awakes or tropical swallows were depositing their eggs. So closely were they located that it was difficult to avoid stepping on the birds or eggs. The disturbed birds rose in the air with a deafening clamor, and the bolder ones darted down and beat at our heads with wings and beaks. It was well for us that they were rather frail birds.

When one of the residents of the island wished to avail himself of a supply of eggs, he went out to the Wide-awake Fair and staked out a lot. After clearing off all the eggs from his claim, he gathered each day the new eggs that were laid. In this way he was assured of fresh eggs. I was told that the wide-awakes returned to the island to breed at intervals of eight months.

Another bird colony that I went to see was on Boatswain Bird Island, a great rock that rises out of the sea close to the east end of Ascension. The place is not very accessible, but a skillful St. Helena boatman landed our party on the base of the rock and we scrambled up a precarious path to the summit. The island gets its name from the boatswain bird, but at the time of my visit the place was almost monopolized by man-of-war birds. As we passed about among the dark somber birds brooding over their eggs, their long-winged, swallow-tailed mates wheeled and circled close overhead staring down with fierce eyes, but they made no attempt to use their formidable hook-tipped beaks.

When the male man-of-war bird takes his turn on the nest he inflates the wattles under his throat until they resemble a pink toy balloon. The female will stay by her nest with great courage, but if the male is on duty, at the approach of a man, he clears out with much flapping of long wings and deflating his balloon as he goes.

After tramping about the lava beds and desert plains for a few days, I found a climb to Green Mountain refreshing. The peak rises to over two thousand eight hundred feet above the sea, and up in the clouds around the summit is a farm where vegetables are grown and a few cattle and sheep find pasturage. Some of the slopes are covered over with cement and form catchment areas where rain water is collected and carried through a pipe line to the large reservoirs in the settlement below.

On the summit of the peak I was shown a lily pond. Around a shallow pool a thicket of bamboos has been planted. The peak has just the proper altitude to pierce the trade wind clouds as they go sailing by, so that much of the time it is enveloped in fog. The moisture condenses on the bamboos and runs down into the pool. It is called a dew pond—something of a novelty for a desert island.

On December 15th, I was ready to sail once more. Harbormaster Drew sent me a crate of vegetables and a bunch of bananas as a memento of the desert isle. A party came out in a motorboat, and gave me a hearty cheer as I cast off the mooring line and sailed away for America. The trade wind was light and the *Islander* made her way leisurely along, accompanied by schools of flying fish and fleets of green Portuguese men-of-war, the latter all decked out with pink trimmings on their sails. Occasionally a school of porpoises broke the monotony.

One night I awoke from a sound sleep and received the shock of my life when I stepped out of my berth into water over the cabin floor. My first thought was that my boat was sinking, but a sound of tinkling water led to the water cask, where a lantern had fallen against the tap and started it. I was relieved to find that I had wakened before the water had all drained out. It would not have been pleasant to have had to begin drinking water out of the bilge before I arrived in the next port. As it was I bailed some ten gallons out of the pump well. There was still an abundant supply left, and the next day I fixed that tap so it would not open so easily.

Fernando Noronha was sighted on December 26th, and attracted by its solitary peak, that appeared to be leaning to one side, I ran close by the island. As I approached, a number of rocks and small islands were seen extending off the north shore. I had no information about the place, but trusting to my eyes to find a way, I ran through among them. I passed through a channel between a prominent white rock and a flat lava island, and so narrow was the place I could have tossed a biscuit on either shore. It did not look too good when rocks began showing right under the keel, but there was no turning back against wind and tide in the narrow channel. With a wave of my hat I swept by a graybearded man, who suddenly appeared on the lava island and stood staring at me. I had a few anxious moments, then I ran clear of the place into deep water. There were buildings on the island and it appeared to be under cultivation, but the only person that I saw about the place was the old man who popped up on the lava island. The leaning peak of Fernando Noronha faded out in the coming night, and the next morning great numbers of sea birds indicated that I was passing the Rocas.

In the region of the equator, which was crossed on December 31st, I ran into light winds accompanied by squalls and much rain. On January 4th, the northeast trade winds came along, blowing strong and kicking up a most uncomfortable chop of sea. Coming right on the beam it made wet sailing, so I shortened the sail and let the *Islander* make the best of it.

In my desire to keep well away from the South American coast, I kept edging to the north until I was nearing the track of steamers going to southern ports, and I saw the funnel and deck load of lumber of a steamer on the northern horizon. In all my voyage I had never met a vessel within hailing distance at sea. I had often wished that I might meet up with a large ship so as to see what the people on board would think of my little craft cruising along in mid-ocean. Along about this time I found out.

It was shortly after midnight on the morning of January 10th. It was a clear night and the moon was full. The wind was blowing fresh and there was a lump of a sea running. The *Islander* was cruising along under jib and mizzensail, and I was down below sound asleep, when we struck something with a crash. I sprang up to see the dark hull of a steamer looming alongside. My first thought was that she had run into my vessel, but she was going on the same course as the *Islander,* and at the same speed. If the crew had seen my boat in time to slow down, why had they not kept away? I threw the tiller over and tried to bring my boat up into the wind, but she was in too close contact. There I was with my boat on the windward side of the steamer, and every sea washing her up and down the iron side. In one of her upward rushes the foremast speared the steamer's bridge. In the bright moonlight I saw a row of faces lined up along the steamer's waist and peering down at me. Just then some one threw a large line, that hit me on the head, and an inquiring voice said, "Have a rope." For a moment I was dazed, and then it began to dawn on me that I was expected to leave my ship and its contents and climb up the rope! Actually they were trying to rescue me.

I was somewhat excited, so my answer was not very polite! "What do I want with your rope?"

An officer on the bridge inquired, "Don't you want assistance?"

"I want you to get out of this, go ahead, back up, or do something !!!!"

About that time a big wave came along, and I thought that I was going to board the steamer and take my ship along with me. For a moment the *Islander* was up on the steamer's rail, then the back-wash from the side of the steamer threw her off, and she came up into the wind and ran clear. As she rounded to into the wind, the steamer came rolling back toward her, striking the end of the mizzen boom and breaking the gooseneck.

I was not alongside more than five minutes, but it was the most thrilling five minutes of my voyage.

As soon as the *Islander* was clear of the steamer, I began to take stock of the damage done. A glance showed that the mizzen rigging was broken, and I let the sail come down. When the mizzen sail was down the *Islander* came round till the jib shivered by the leach. That finished the bowsprit that had been broken, and the jib came drifting alongside. The steamer was moving ahead by this time, and the *Islander* drifted off astern with all sail doused and roll-ing so violently that with the jib stay gone, I thought she would jump the foremast out. I ran forward, gathered in the jib and broken bowsprit, and with all speed began to set up the jib stay at the stem head. While I was occupied with this task, the steamer backed into hailing distance and I learned that she was an oil transport bound for Buenos Aires. Her name I did not get, though an officer called it out several times. I gave them the name and home port of my boat, and they afterwards reported the meeting. They asked repeatedly if I wanted to be taken off, but I was not going to Buenos Aires just then, so they blew their whistle and steamed away on their course.

They had, no doubt, come up with the best of intentions, but I would have appreciated the call more if they had sounded their whistle first and then come alongside with my little boat in their lee.

When I had the jib stay set up the best I could, the small jib was put on, and we drifted along on the course. I was tired and turned into my berth, but the excitement of speaking my first ship at sea was too much and I did not sleep. When morning came, I spliced the broken mizzen rigging and put on the reefed mizzen. With this sail I ran on until the next day when the weather calmed down a little. I then hove to with the mizzen sail and went to work to set up the jib stay more securely.

A short bowsprit was made out of the broken one. After cutting off the broken end and refitting it in place, the bowsprit extended two feet and eight inches instead of the original six feet. All the while as I lay out on the new bowsprit splicing in the wire bobstay, a yellow and brown spotted shark swam around underneath, apparently watching me. As a species that I had not seen before, he interested me greatly, but if he was expecting me to furnish him his dinner, he was disappointed.

This short bowsprit was not long enough to use the

large jib, but there was room for the proper setting of the small or storm jib, and when the jib stay was set taut to it the foremast was as secure as ever. When the job was finished, the reefed mainsail was set, and we began to move along once more.

My course was now to Trinidad Island. The trade wind had backed round to east by north, and for several days I was running before it with a following sea that was altogether out of proportion to the strength of the wind, though it was strong and squally at times. With only the small jib the *Islander* was not carrying enough head sail, and constant watching was required to keep her from broaching to. At night, when I wanted to sleep, I had to take off all the after sail, consequently I was slow about getting into port.

On the morning of January 18th after a night of wind and rain, the *Islander* was cruising along under easy sail, and I was keeping a good lookout for land. The sea was running high with an extra big roller coming along every few minutes. When one of the big ones began to lift the *Islander,* she would gather headway like a toboggan going downhill, and, as the crest caught up with her, only quick work at the tiller kept her from broaching to. For a moment she would seem to stand balancing in the mass of foam on the summit and then fall off on the after slope of the wave and lose headway only to be caught up once more by the following wave. But the wind and sea were going down, and the sky was clearing. Before noon Tobago Island was sighted, while off to the southwest a great cloud bank lay over Trinidad. When night came on I was sailing over a smooth sea between the two islands with lights showing on either hand. At sunrise a squall came sweeping along, and the *Islander* went tearing away before it, while I could scarce see beyond the bowsprit end for the blinding rain. When it had passed, the three small islands at the entrance to the Gulf of Paria were close at hand. Under the lee of the land the wind was almost cut off, and for most of the day the *Islander* was just stemming the current in the pass, but in the end she won through and came out into the wind blowing strong across the gulf. At sunset I anchored in the lee of a small island. The scene was beautiful, and the name of the pass, "Dragon's Mouth," did not seem appropriate. Beyond the little islet lay the valleys and mountains of Trinidad where the dark green forests were splotched with the red groves of immortelle trees in bloom. As darkness settled down, I lay on deck watching the fireflies among the trees on the islet whose branches seemed to overhang the *Islander,* so close to the shore did she lie. I was off again at sunrise, and began beating up against the east wind toward Port of Spain. The wind was light when I started, but a squall was under way when I arrived; so the battered *Islander* came in with a flourish, and the anchor was dropped near the customhouse about noon on January 20, 1925.

The boarding officer was at a loss to know how to proceed when he found that I had no clearance papers and had not brought a bill of health from my last port.

After a little good-natured banter, it was decided that, as I had been thirty-five days at sea and was still in good health, it was all right. When this question was settled the collector of customs, Thomas Cutler, sent a launch to bring my craft to a berth at the custom-house wharf, where she lay while I was seeing the sights of the charming island.

I don't remember ever having been so sea-weary as I was when I arrived at Port of Spain. Any place with a solid foundation would have been appreciated then, and here I was at gorgeous Trinidad. It was a land of plenty, and I first turned my attention to the market where a great variety of fruits and vegetables were displayed. A long-continued diet of prunes had given me a wonderful appetite for oranges.

To me there is a wonderful fascination about seeing a strange island for the first time, and approaching it alone, as I did, was next thing to discovering the place. I had little information about Trinidad other than that it was the place where pitch comes from. Now my reason for calling at Trinidad instead of Barbados, was that, while I was looking over some old charts, which were given me by Mr. Alfred Hall at Mauritius, I came across one of Trinidad Island. The chart was the deciding factor, but Trinidad proved to be one of the most interesting places of all.

It was good to be on the ground and in the shade of the trees once more. The island was like a new botanical garden to me. There are some famous drives in and around Port of Spain, and the hospitable residents saw to it that I did not go away without seeing them. There was one scene that I remember above all the rest. With a party of island friends I was enjoying a drive. Sunset had tempered the heat of the day, and it was dusk when we glided into a beautiful winding road through a grove of bowery trees where myriads of fireflies danced among the branches. It was like drifting through a land of enchantment.

As a rule people living in the tropics don't walk when it can be avoided, but one of my Trinidad friends, Mr. Gerold, enjoyed going with me for long hikes in the hills and woods and gave me much information about the country that I would otherwise have missed. One gets more intimately acquainted with the country when walking than in any other way.

Of the places that I liked best in Trinidad, there was a glen among the hills, where, from a mass of overhanging tropical foliage, a waterfall poured into a tiny lake that was called Blue Basin. Then there was a deep shaded ravine, its steep banks draped with ferns and moss, through which my friend Gerold and I wended our way to a little bay on the north shore.

It was the season for tourists in the West Indies, and when one of the great seagoing hotels that rushed from place to place called in at Port of Spain, I was kept busy answering questions about my craft and myself. As the passengers from the steamers were landed at the customhouse wharf, the diminutive *Islander* flying the American flag attracted some attention, and many of the tourists paused to see what we were like and to exchange travel notes. How one could make so long a voyage in so small a vessel was no end of wonder to most of them, and they asked innumerable questions about how I managed it, and especially about my food and water supply. One man, after gazing long and pensively at my craft, asked, "What do you do for milk?" I explained that it was a case of being weaned before I left home, which answer seemed to amuse the rest of the party. And milk wasn't the only thing I had to use a substitute for. However, the most of this world that was worth exploring was discovered before the days of steam heat and artificial refrigeration. Among the tourists I met some very interesting people, and sometimes I went with them to view the wonders of a tourist ship. We ascended and descended in elevators, saw the swimming pool, the golf course, and glass-enclosed sun parlor. For invalids and elderly ladies I had to admit that the apartments on the steamer had many advantages, but I soon tired of looking at the sea through a window, and up on the bridge the sea was so far away that I felt lonesome. I liked my way of seeing the world best, and sometimes one of the tourists confided that he envied me my independent way of voyaging.

Carnival is the main event of the year in Port of Spain. For two days the populace thronged the streets and masked revelers in fantastic costumes paraded. Many of the costumes were good, but what struck me was the number of small black boys made up to represent the Wild West characters of the movies.

When the carnival was over, I went to work to repair the battered *Islander.* I bought a stick of native wood with which to fashion a new bowsprit, and my friend Gerold, who was in the hardware business, produced wire and other material to replace the broken rigging. The job attracted plenty of interested spectators, and I gathered the impression that the native workmen did not like the idea of a white man doing work of this kind, but some one passed the word that I was doing the voyage as a stunt, and one of the conditions was that I was to do everything myself. They were then content to stand around and see how I did the job. I answered many questions about the work and stopped often to entertain tourists, but at last the *Islander* came out in even better trim than before those well-meaning seamen attempted to take me off her in mid-ocean. When I had covered all with a new coat of paint only a scar on her side remained to show where she struck on the steamer's rail. After all, it would be a monotonous voyage if there were no adventures mixed with it.

One has not done justice to the sights of Trinidad until he has been to the Pitch Lake, so, when I had finished repairing the *Islander,* I sailed for Brighton. The run of some twenty miles down the shore was uneventful except for a terrific downpour of rain that lasted for an hour or two, when I learned that it could rain as hard in Trinidad as it does in Samoa.

The Pitch Lake, some one hundred and fourteen acres in extent, is but a few minutes' walk from the Brighton Pier. It is not a very picturesque sight, but on close inspection is rather an interesting place. The hot tropical sun pouring down on the black surface makes it one of the hottest spots in the world. The surface is hard enough to bear foot traffic, while a wooden corduroy road carries a wire tram that transports the pitch, or asphalt, to vessels for shipment to all parts of the world. Gas bubbles rising through the pitch, keep it in a state of slow ebullition, giving rise to creases that divide the surface into patches somewhat resembling alligator leather. The rain water that collects in the creases, or wrinkles, though almost steaming hot, swarms with minute fishes that prey on the larvæ of mosquitoes. These same pools of warm water make admirable washtubs for the colored women, who came there to do their laundry.

Sir Walter Raleigh calked his ships with pitch from the lake in 1595, and enough has been taken out since to lower the surface more than fifteen feet. An estimate of the amount still left in the deposit was being made at the time. For this purpose the depth was being measured at several places by driving a steam-heated pipe through to the bottom. I was told by the foreman in charge of the work that at the location which they were then sounding they were down to one hundred and ninety feet and still going.

After seeing the Pitch Lake and the oil wells in the

vicinity, I sailed to Scotland Bay, a sheltered cove near the entrance to the Gulf of Paria. At the first favorable tide I ran the *Islander* on the beach for cleaning and painting the bottom. Colonel Carey, a retired British army officer, was living on the shore, and he and his two young sons turned to and assisted with the work. With so many hands to help, the work was play except for one incident. I was wading barefoot in the water around the yawl when I stepped on something that seemed to pierce my heel to the bone. The pain was intense and my leg ached to the knee, though the wound was too small to be seen and no blood came from it. Young Carey said it was a small fish that lay concealed in the sand with its poisonous dorsal spine ready for business. He had once stepped on one himself. There was no inflammation or swelling of my foot, but it was several days before the pain subsided, and there was a very sensitive spot on my heel for more than a month.

One night while at anchor in Scotland Bay, I was sitting on deck cooling off after a warm day, when a school of small fish broke the surface of the water alongside the yawl. Immediately some strange shapes fluttered down from above, intent on catching the fish. It was too dark for me to tell what they were, but when I spoke to the Careys about them, I was told that they were fish-eating bats. They said that when they were casting a net for fish at night, the bats were so intent on catching the fish that the evil-smelling creatures sometimes became entangled in the net and were drawn in along with the fish. A fish-eating bat was another new one for me.

From Scotland Bay I sailed to near-by Gasparee Island, where many Trinidad people come to spend their holidays and week-ends in the pretty bungalows and villas they have built on its shores. For a few days I rested at this quiet resort, being entertained by and receiving the calls of the people on shore. Many of the merry boys and girls arrived alongside swimming, for the bathing was excellent.

Returning to Port of Spain, I took on supplies and water, had a last word with the friends who had shown so much kindness to the *Islander* while she was recovering from her wounds, and then on April 18, 1925, I sailed for the Panama Canal. The wind was light, and evening found me drifting off Scotland Bay, so I anchored and renewed my acquaintance with Colonel Carey and family. It was noon the next day before the breeze came up. I did a turn around the bay, so that Colonel Carey might get a photograph of the *Islander* under sail, and then stood off to pass by Monos Island, where I again ran into a calm. Mr. A. Baxter, who was stopping at one of the bungalows on the island, came off in a rowboat and joined me while I drifted.

Mr. Baxter was a world-wide traveler, whose path, by some strange coincidence, had here crossed the track of the *Islander* for the third time. We first met in Tahiti, and then, after devious wanderings, he popped up in Fiji while I was there. When I was repairing the *Islander* at Port of Spain, he had paused on a tour of the South American continent and come to see relatives living on Trinidad. As we "gammed," a breeze came round the point of the island. Mr. Baxter went back to the bungalow among the trees, and the *Islander* sailed out into the Caribbean Sea.

A course was laid to pass to the north of all of the islands off the South American coast, and I saw none of them, though vast numbers of sea birds flying about indicated that I was passing near. There were gannets, man-of-war birds, petrels, and wide-awakes. Twice I saw lumber-laden steamers passing on the northern horizon. Remembering the tank steamer, I wished they were farther away. On April 25th I passed to the south of the sun once more. The wind was light but on the tenth day out I discovered Panama when some misty looking hills appeared in the southwest.

I had neither chart or sailing directions for the land I was approaching but I sailed on until midnight when I ran into a downpour of rain. The wind died out, but the rain continued till dawn. When it was daylight, I saw that I was close to some small islands that were scattered along a line of reefs. Breakers flashed and boomed all along the reefs, and I was closer in than I wanted to be. Everything was so shrouded in clouds and mist that it was some time before I could make out the situation. The trade wind that had carried me across the Atlantic Ocean was now dying down, and all day I drifted close by the San Blas Islands. A light breeze came up in the afternoon and for a time it seemed as if I were going to get clear of the place, but the breeze failed and a head current set me right back to where I had been in the morning.

Many times I have been asked if I did not forget how to talk when sailing alone. Well, there is no fear of it. Situations like the one I was now in stimulate the memory most wonderfully.

There was a downpour of rain again during the night, but a fair breeze came out of the northeast with the dawn and the reefs were soon left behind. During the day I saw boats sailing along the shore and smoke rising from among the trees. Late in the afternoon I rounded the lighthouse on Manzanillo Point and things began to liven up, and several steamers in sight at the same time indicated that I was now on one of the great highways of commerce. Night settled down while I was still a long way out. My information about the harbor at Cristobal was limited to what I could glean from *The Pocket Guide to the West Indies,* so when I saw the harbor lights blinking, I hove to and waited for daylight. In the early morning of May 2nd, the *Islander* passed the breakwater with a great gray steamer following close in her wake. With the vast bulk of the steamer looming far above her mainmast the *Islander* seemed smaller than ever, but she had put another ocean behind.

XIV

Panama and Home

IT was the morning of May 2nd, when I arrived at
Cristobal. No one cared to look at the bill of
health that I had brought from Port of Spain, but the
business of measuring the *Islander* for the purpose of
fixing the canal toll went forward at once. I did not
care to pass through the canal that day but went on
shore to look around.

What struck me at once was the pace at which things
were being done. I was in America once more, though
I can't say that it impressed me favorably at that time.
I had fallen into a habit of moving leisurely myself.
Port officials and others that I met were very obliging
and afforded me any assistance in their power.

I went first to the post office, and among letters
from California was a clipping from a Los Angeles
newspaper, containing an interview with Captain Johnson, of the S. S. *San Quirino,* an oil transport plying
between Los Angeles and Buenos Aires. It seems that
it was the *San Quirino* that brushed up against the
Islander off the South American coast, and Captain
Johnson had arrived back at Los Angeles while the
Islander was undergoing repairs at the dreamy isle.
According to the report Captain Johnson mistook the

Islander for a derelict, and approached so closely as to almost swamp her.

After my return to Los Angeles, the *San Quirino* arrived in port again. Captain Johnson was not in command at that time, but I called on the other members of the crew and we had a jolly good laugh while recounting the incident. The first officer said it was he who threw the rope up which I was expected to climb and abandon my ship. He also remembered what I had said to him on that occasion.

As I was coming on shore I noticed a strange looking ketch alongside the landing. Later in the day I met Captain X——, and went on board his craft, the *Big Bill*. He had built his boat in a penny arcade at Chicago, and accounted for its peculiar sheer with saying that there was not room in the place to build according to the original plan. I learned how the *Big Bill* had sailed from Chicago with a party of scientists on board, bound on a voyage of investigation to some distant tropic isles. While the *Big Bill* was dropping down the Illinois and Mississippi rivers and then across the Gulf of Mexico, the scientists dropped off one by one, and Captain X—— arrived at Cristobal with his wife and small son for a crew. His difficulty now was to collect funds with which to carry on while seeing the beautiful islands. The small boy was taking advantage of his opportunities and seemed to be getting more out of the adventure than any one else.

A few days after my arrival, Mr. Jacob Goldberg, whom I had last seen aboard the *Los Amigos* in Los

THE WATER IS FINE AT GASPAREE, A SEASIDE RESORT NEAR
PORT OF SPAIN, TRINIDAD.

Photograph by Lewis

THE ISLANDER IS SIGHTED FROM THE OLD SPANISH FORT AT
PORTO BELLO BAY, PANAMA.

THE ISLANDER HOMEWARD-BOUND THROUGH THE PANAMA CANAL.

Left: ALAIN GERBAULT *and* HARRY PIDGEON *on board the Firecrest at Balboa, May 12, 1925.*

Right: E. W. SCRIPPS *and* HARRY PIDGEON *on board the Ohio at Balboa, June 16, 1925.*

Angeles Harbor, came over from Balboa to renew our acquaintance and tell me of his voyage down the west coast. Owing to the revolution in Mexico, they had found trouble and no profit there. They had had an amusing search for hidden treasure in Central America, but brought no gold to the surface. The partnership was dissolved at Amapala, and after devious wanderings, Goldberg, with a Costa Rican boy for a crew, brought the *Los Amigos* to Balboa. There he sold his boat and found employment as a mechanical draftsman with the Canal Commission. He had another dream ship in mind, and when he has mended his fortune hopes to be afloat once more. His Costa Rican mate had found work as a boatman, and was waiting to join him in any further voyages he might undertake.

I was making some inquiries about Porto Bello, the scene of the last exploit of Sir Frances Drake, when I met Mr. Lewis, a Panama photographer. He proposed joining me in an excursion to some points of historic interest in the vicinity. Mr. Lewis brought along an outboard motor which we attached to the stern of the *Islander* in an attempt to turn her into a motorboat. In smooth water and no wind it pushed her along at about three miles an hour, but the rise and fall of the *Islander's* stern in even a slight swell was enough alternately to lift the propeller out of the water and then drown the motor. However, it sometimes helped us to get to an anchorage when we were becalmed.

One of our objects had been to visit and get photo-

graphs of the San Blas Indians, but, owing to the ob-
jections of the Panamanian authorities, we were not
able to do so. Mr. Lewis was acquainted with the
Indians, but things were a bit unsettled just then. It
seems that a short time before some colored police had
been stationed on the San Blas Islands, and these
worthies had tried out some of their own theories
about civilizing Indians. As a result the Indians had
turned to and wiped out the lot of them, a fate they
most likely deserved.

At Porto Bello we found a few rusty, corrugated
iron huts standing amid the ruins of the old Spanish
fort—all that was left to mark the site of what had
once been a place of such wealth and affluence as to
attract, in turn, the attention of Drake, Morgan, and
Vernon. There was not much to see there, but it was
good to look over the scene.

We did not get much use out of the motor on our
cruise, but it came in handy after all. While the canal
officials were kind and ready to assist me in every way,
they were prejudiced in regard to sailing craft. For
the purpose of passing through the canal the *Islander*
was rated at five tons, and the charges were five
dollars for measuring and three dollars and seventy-
five cents for canal toll. This was certainly reasonable
enough but hiring a launch at five dollars an hour to
tow the *Islander* through the canal was a matter for
serious consideration for one who had been away from
home as long as I had. Right here my friend Goldberg, late skipper of the *Los Amigos,* came to my

assistance. The outboard motor still remained on the *Islander,* and Goldberg had a license to run a motor-boat on the canal. He joined me on board at Cristo-bal and the *Islander,* along with the steamer *Orinoco,* passed onto the locks to be lifted up into Gatun Lake. When we reached the upper level, a smart breeze was blowing. As the *Orinoco* was passing out of the locks, her bow lines were cast off and she swung round in the wind and grounded in the entrance, where she stuck until a line was run out with which to haul her off. When the *Orinoco* was clear, the outboard motor re-fused to do its work, so the *Islander* spread her wings and sailed out into the lake with a flourish. For a few days she lay at anchor at Gatun, while I watched the procession of great ships passing through the canal. Of the ships that passed that way none interested half so much as the *Tusitala,* one of the last of Amer-ica's square-rigged windjammers. With her sails furled and at the end of a towline, she was still the most impressive sight that I saw while there.

Mr. Goldberg had arranged to meet me at the other end of the lake on the following week-end, so on Friday morning I set sail. The wind was light and there were many changes, but it was a delightful sail among the green islands of Gatun Lake. When the lake was formed by the construction of the great dam at Gatun, the trees were only cleared from the ship channel, so much of the lake is obstructed. But for the dead branches of the drowned forest standing above the sur-face, the lake would be a lovely place for small boat sailing. Its many islands and the surrounding hills are green with strange and beautiful trees, while the numerous coves and inlets would form enchanting places for exploration. At the end of a most enjoyable day I came to where the lake became a narrow channel and anchored for the night. The next morning I was under way again, and soon after met Mr. Goldberg, who came out from Gamboa in a canoe to meet me. Mr. Goldberg knew something about such things, so was able to coax the motor into life, and we entered the great cut that connects Gatun Lake with Pacific waters. We arrived at the Pedro Miguel Locks along with a big ore carrier, and along with it were lowered into Miraflores Lake. As we were leaving the locks, the motor went on a strike so I put on the canvas, and went for a sail on this very beautiful little lake, the prettiest spot along the canal. By the time the motor was going again, we had lost our turn with the ore ship, but a Norwegian freighter was following close after, and we were lowered from Miraflores Lake to the Pacific level along with her. We were soon through, and the motor purred merrily as it pushed the *Islander* out into the salt water of the Pacific. I felt some elation at being so near home again. We soon came to Balboa where the harbormaster gave us a mooring close by the landing.

At Balboa, when I arrived, was Alain Gerbault, a Frenchman who had crossed the Atlantic Ocean single-handed in the cutter *Firecrest*. He sailed for the South Seas soon after I arrived, but I had the pleasure of meeting Gerbault on board the *Firecrest,* and he inspected the *Islander.* I enjoyed meeting this courageous seaman very much, for those who have had similar experiences understand each other better. However, I did not fancy the *Firecrest* for single-handed cruising. As a racing cutter, the purpose for which she was designed, she was probably all right, but she was certainly not designed for the comfort of the man at the helm, there being neither cockpit nor coaming for his protection. From what I learned he had had a hard passage, one that would have discouraged most amateurs. For a tender he had a folding canvas boat that did not look very substantial for use among coral reefs, but I think he was a strong swimmer. After seeing the *Islander* he said he liked the *Firecrest* better, so we were both satisfied with our outfit and equipment.

If a seafaring man lingers in the Canal Zone he will likely meet up with some old acquaintances. A few days after my arrival at Balboa, I noticed a large power yacht alongside the wharf. It had a familiar appearance and on investigating I found it to be the same *Ohio* that had crossed the track of the *Islander* once before at Thursday Island. The owner, Mr. E. W. Scripps, was surprised to see me again as he had heard that the old sea had gotten the *Islander* and her crew. He had circled the world since I had seen him last and had called in again at Thursday Island and Port Moresby, and at both places I had been reported among the missing. He asked many questions about my movements after sailing from Thursday Island, but more than anything else he was interested in how economical it was for me to sail single-handed. He related some incidents of his early struggles in the newspaper business, when it had been necessary for him to sail close to the wind himself. I venture to say that his expenses for a week aboard the *Ohio* would have covered my whole venture with the *Islander,* but I think he realized that I was getting more out of it than he was. When I bubbled over with enthusiasm about places that I had seen, he said he was sick of scenery and that he had not gone ashore at half the places where he had called. He went to sea because he did not feel well on land. My coming on board put him in a good humor, and he had his secretary make some photographs of himself and me together, saying it would make him famous. The old gentleman was nearing the end of his voyage. Soon after I arrived at my home port word came that he had died on board the *Ohio* off the coast of Africa.

There was usually something interesting in the way of yachts at Balboa. In the wake of the *Ohio* the British yacht *St. George* came in with a party of archæologists who had been trying to solve the mystery of the huge stone images on Easter Island. A little later the *Arcturus,* with Dr. William Beebe and staff, arrived from the Galapagos Islands. According to my friend T——, of the harbormaster's office, Balboa was a sort of clearing house for scientific expeditions, and he contemplated bringing out a book entitled, *Scientists We Have Known.* I believe he was a bit of a wag.

For a few days the harbor was crowded with United States warships, mostly destroyers, coming from maneuvers in the Pacific. Thousands of smart young seamen thronged the streets of Balboa and Panama City, buying up the available stock of monkeys and parrots. Taking into consideration the number of these creatures I saw carried away from Port of Spain and Panama by tourists and the United States Navy, there must be an inexhaustible supply. Occasionally a dealer passed off a parrakeet on one of the unsuspecting boys in blue for a parrot. One young bluejacket passing on his way to his ship with an adult parrakeet, about the size of a sparrow, remarked, "I'll bet he'll be a great talker, when he grows up."

A party of young men from the U. S. S. *Wyoming,* who were interested in small boat sailing, paid me a visit on board the *Islander* and in turn showed me over their great ship and explained the working of the intricate machinery. One of them was planning for a boat of his own when his days in the navy were done, and then he would go sailing away on a dream voyage. Some day the *Islander* may meet a sister ship with one of these dreamers at the helm.

As soon as I had an opportunity, I went out to see something of the land around me. The business of Balboa and Ancon pertain entirely to the operation of the canal, but they are models that may be studied with advantage by the municipal authorities of any tropical country. They are beautifully laid out along the slopes at the base of Ancon Hill, with plenty of open spaces, green lawns, and noble shade trees. If for no other reason, I would have loved them for the absence of the network of overhanging electric wires that usually makes hideous the skyline of small cities, these necessary appendages of civilization being here confined to underground conduits, where they belong.

It was the rainy season and the weather was sultry, but I usually made my sight-seeing excursions on foot. The view from Ancon Hill is very fine and lured me to the summit several times. From this elevation a wonderful panorama of the Pacific end of the canal extends from Gold Hill on one side to Taboga Island, and the ships coming in from and going out to sea on the other, with Miraflores Locks and Balboa Harbor in between. At the foot of the hill and extending all around it, Balboa, Ancon, and Panama City lay spread out like a map. On a clear day one can see a ruined tower rising above the trees on the lowlands far down the shore. It marks the site where Panama City was located before the buccaneers passed that way.

Mr. C. A. McGlade, a resident of the Canal Zone, came with his auto and put in a day showing me around the country. One of the places that we visited was old Panama, the most picturesque ruin on the isthmus. For this bit of interesting scenery we can thank Sir Henry Morgan, he having rounded out a very colorful career as a buccaneer by sacking the place. The land around about is low and flat, and at low tide a mud flat extends for a mile or so on the sea front. The Spaniard was probably wise when he set fire to and abandoned his city on the approach of the buccaneers, and later rebuilt on a more healthful location.

Occasionally, when I had nothing else to do, I went for a stroll through Panama City. American sanitary engineers have worked their will on the place, but there are some picturesque features left. If the number of women selling tickets on the streets is any criterion, the Panamanian lottery would seem to be the most thriving business of the day. The place that interested me most was the market where gathered the cosmopolitan population, their various hues differing almost as much as the fruits that were being bought and sold. The market is on the waterfront, and most of the produce arrives in boats. From the sea wall I looked out on a hundred tattered sails swaying lazily over dark hulls of strange and varied lines. On the beach a motley crowd of Indians and mestizos were landing their canoes heaped with mangoes and bananas.

There is much of interest to be seen on one's first visit to the Canal Zone, but eventually I made ready for sea again.

I sailed over to Farfan Point, where there is a sandy spot, and beached the *Islander* alongside of some abandoned French dredging machinery. Apparently she was as sound as the day when she sailed on the long voyage, and I had only to spread another coat of copper paint on her bottom. As there is near eighteen feet of tide at the Pacific end of the canal, this is an ideal place for this work, and I have never finished the job of cleaning and painting so easily elsewhere. At the end of the second day I was back at the mooring, and ready to begin taking on stores.

The cookstove that had been in use since the *Islander* was launched, was well rusted and burned out, so I replaced it with another from the canal commissary department, and I did not neglect to take on a good supply of wood for fuel. For the oil stove that I occasionally used, and for use in the lamps, I took on fifteen gallons of kerosene. The voyage home, from all information I could gather, promised to be a long one, so I laid in provisions to last several months and filled all available containers with water.

While I was engaged in this task, a black lizard, more than a foot in length, came on board and took up its abode. Where it came from I did not know, but, at the time, an old Panamanian craft was attached to the same mooring as the *Islander*. I presume it came from that vessel by way of the mooring lines. It hid away in the hold, but at midday, when a shaft of sunlight poured down the companionway, it came out to sun itself on the cabin floor. I tried to be friendly, but whenever I came near it retreated underneath the water cask. The lizard was going to sea with me, but if it would catch cockroaches, I was not going to object. So long as I was in the tropics I was never able to get entirely rid of the cockroaches, though I trapped them continually with a Mason jar, baited with pieces of fruit or vegetables. Even a little fresh water in the jar had a great attraction for them.

The *Islander's* old sails were not improved by their stay in the heat and damp of the Canal Zone. Except for the run from Durban to Cape Town, they had been in use since the *Islander* was launched, and if I had had no others they would have served for the rest of the voyage, but there are some things that I like better than sewing old sails, so her best suit was bent on.

To the west of Panama and the Central American coast is a vast region of light winds and calms, varied by squalls of wind and rain. Of this region the sailing directions say: "The passage to the westward during the rainy season is a tedious affair. It often occurs that twenty miles of westing are not made in a week, and it is only by the industrious use of every squall and slant of wind that the passage can be made."

On August 7th I stood out to sea on the longest run of the voyage and what proved to be the most difficult part of all. A light northerly wind carried us out of Panama Bay, and I passed Cape Mala at noon on the second day. Here I parted company with the stream of steam traffic passing through the Panama Canal and bore away to the southwest alone. After sunset the wind came round to southwest, and I stood off to south. There was rain during the night but morning came with clear weather and light wind from west by south in which I drifted on to the southward. Extracts from the log of the *Islander* show the leisurely way in which we traversed this region:

Monday, August 10.—Warm with light wind in the forenoon. Had a bath in the sea during a calm.

Latitude at noon 6° 21′ north.

Longitude 81° 30′ west.

Wind came stronger afternoon. After sunset flashes of lightning were seen on the horizon and the sky looked squally. While watching a dark cloud that was forming to windward, I became aware of a great luminous patch of water around the yawl. It gave me a sensation of awe at first, but later I made it out to be small fishes swimming along below the surface. Later they swam away to another part of the sea.

Tuesday, August 11.—Squall came up in the latter part of the night and I lowered the mains'l: put it up again later. During the morning the wind came up strong, and as we were close-hauled water began coming on board. I put two reefs in the main and for a time needed it. Rained hard. At noon the wind died out but the drizzle kept on. A shark followed us for a time during the afternoon. Saw a yellow and black sea snake. Wind strong late in the afternoon but died out after nightfall. Yawl rolling something awful.

The United States weather chart indicates the prevailing wind in this part of the sea to be from the southwest. Where the southeast trade wind extends to north of the equator it has a tendency to come round to southwest. When I met this southwest monsoon I tried for a time to stand west, but the wind was too light, and close-hauled into it the progress was not encouraging, and meeting with the equatorial countercurrent, I drifted off to the north and farther into the doldrums. In this sultry region there was a rain squall in sight most of the time, and at times we drifted about with wet sails slatting in a drizzle, but occasionally there was a fine day.

Monday, August 17.—Day dawned calm with just a few clouds on the horizon. Light breeze came up after sunrise. Drifting along all day with wind from south to southwest.

Latitude at noon 7° 06' north.

Longitude 87° 15' west.

Have a school of fish for company. A pair of sharks paid us a visit. See many jellyfish and some water insects.

Tuesday, August 18.—Ran through the night with all sails set. Calm at sunrise but light wind came up out of north. During the forenoon a turtle came up under the stern of the yawl, and as the wind was light, it swam along for a time underneath. I could hear its hard shell bumping the bottom. The wind came stronger and it was left behind. It had a large wound on its neck and several small fishes attached to it as one often sees them attached to sharks.

Latitude at noon 7° 24' north.

Longitude 87° 20' west.

Changed course to southwest. Wind died out in the evening and left us rolling. Rain squall after nightfall and breeze came out of west.

My observations on the last two days indicated that I had only made about five miles westing and had gone north about eighteen miles though I had been sailing west for the twenty-four hours at an estimated speed of two miles per hour. During the next two days I gained about thirty miles westing and went north about thirteen miles. The equatorial countercurrent was getting too strong. I now saw that I must stand farther to the south and into the southeast trade winds. As the prevailing breeze varied from west to south, I stood off to south whenever I could do so without losing too much westing. If the wind came to south, I stood off to southwest.

About this time the black lizard that had come forth each day when the sun was shining to bask in its rays failed to appear, and I never saw it again. No doubt it had become disgusted with the length of the voyage and the fare it was getting and abandoned ship. But I had other company. On the way out from Panama Bay, a school of small fishes had attached themselves to the *Islander* and were following in her wake. There were twenty or more of them, six inches to a foot in length and all striped like zebras. They kept close up to the stern, lagging behind a few yards when the *Islander* quickened her pace with a puff of wind; then speeding up they would pass out of sight under the hull. They kept the same position day after day. I presume fishes never sleep, but must be on the alert for their enemies day and night. It is eat and be eaten with them.

Thursday, August 20.—Wind light, only enough to give steerageway. Sea quite calm, and wonderful sky flecked with light clouds. Saw several turtles, one of which for a time swam in the wake of the *Islander*.

Latitude at noon 7° 37' north.

Wind came out of west by north in the evening and course was changed to southwest.

Friday, August 21.—Stood all night to southwest. Wind coming stronger to-day. Still standing to southwest and hope to get better winds farther south.

Saturday, August 22.—Woke up in the midst of a squall. Wind coming from all about. Let the mains'l come down, but the disturbance soon passed. After it was over I stood away to south once more. Rain squall in the forenoon. Caught a little water and had a bath in the rain.

Latitude at noon 6° 39′ north.

Longitude 88° 30′ west.

Seem to be getting out of the current somewhat. Wind came out of southwest and very light during the afternoon. Drifting off to south or west by turns. School of dolphins joined us. Rain squall at dusk, after which wind came out of south by west.

I was sitting drowsily at the tiller when the dolphins came up with a rush. For a few minutes they made the water boil around the stern. As they darted in and out, their dorsal fins seemed to hiss through the surface of the sea. Barring the killer whale (orca) the dolphin, in action, is the most ferocious looking creature that I have ever seen. In a few moments they settled down and for a time swam quietly alongside. I got out a trolling hook but they did not care for it and seemed to be fed up. The school of little striped fishes that had been swimming in the wake were never seen again.

A few days later I saw a man-of-war bird hovering over a turtle. When I was closer, the turtle appeared to be dead and floating with its back well out of water.

It was surrounded by small fishes, or what appeared to be fishes, which were trying to escape the rushes of a large fish that was making a meal of them. In their struggles to save themsclves some of them slid up the sloping back of the turtle till they were out of the water. The man-of-war hawk was picking these small fry off their perch.

Down through the region of rain squalls and calms the *Islander* edged her way to west and south until she came out into the southeast trade winds.

Sunday, September 6.—Squalls with rain. Observation of sun at noon not good. Wind more fair, south by east. Wind fresh and stars coming out after nightfall.

Monday, September 7.—Weather looking stormy and sky partially overcast. Wind still south by east and strong.

Latitude at noon 3° 43′ north.

Longitude 99° 30′ west.

Wind came stronger in the afternoon and I close-reefed the sails and set the small jib. Changed the course to west. Wet going, but the yawl keeps on her course with little or no attention.

For several days the *Islander* plowed her way through a rough sea with the wind on the beam. I had no proper waterproof garment, so I was content to stay below in the dry and let my ship go to westward under short sail. We had reached into the trades at last and the latitude of 3° 43′ north, observed on September 7, was the farthest south on the run. The bottom was by this time taking on a thick crop of sea barnacles so that our speed was much retarded.

Thursday, September 10.—Rough night and little sleep. Sea rough and wind still strong this morning but weather clearing.

Latitude at noon 3° 59' north.

Longitude 103° 15' west.

Wind began to lull after noon and I shook out a reef of the mains'l. At sunset, I was surprised to see a small freight steamer that passed about two miles astern. Wind and sea going down after nightfall.

Friday, September 11.—Wind light during the night. Beautiful day with a good breeze from south. Best day of the run so far.

Latitude at noon 3° 53' north.

Longitude 104° 15' west.

Had all sail set afternoon. As there were many dolphins and albacore playing about I brought out a trolling hook and tried to add something to the larder. The albacore took the hook almost as soon as it hit the water. In a few minutes I had six in the cockpit. I immediately set to work and cut them up and hung the flesh in the mizzen rigging, to see if it would dry.

Out in the trade winds, where the weather was clear and dry, it seemed that I might be able to preserve some of the fish while they were plentiful. The voyage seemed likely to draw out to such length that food itself might become an object.

Saturday, September 12.—Wind south and good. Cloudy at sunrise but soon cleared. First thing in the morning I tried for fish and caught a large dolphin. After it was tired fighting I landed it with the gaff hook. It was still lively enough and almost jumped out of the cockpit. A most wonderful fish for its build and changing colors, silver then gold, blue, green, and brown. As they swim alongside at night they appear slightly luminous. This one had a squid in its stomach of a kind that was new to me.

My local time watch stopped for a few minutes since yesterday, and the sun had already passed the meridian when I observed for latitude. Saw three whale, or the same one three times, cruising slowly along and passing quite close. Many birds. Longitude by sunset 105° 30'.

Saturday, September 13.—Wind held all through the night but fell light at dawn. Still from south. There was a school of dolphins swimming close alongside with dorsal fins cutting the surface. I tried for them with the gaff hook, hooked the first one and landed it in cockpit. Tried again, and hooked one so vigorous that it took the gaff out of my hand and hurled it twenty or thirty feet away. Wore around and went back to recover it. Only the tip of the handle was above water, and I lost sight of it while coming about so I failed to get it.

Wind breezed up and we moved along good with all sails set.

Latitude at noon 3° 51' north.

Longitude 107° 0' west.

Declination of the sun was 3° 47', so the sun has now passed to the south of us once more. Wind came on to blow at sunset and I tied two reefs in the mains'l.

Tuesday, September 15.—Wind south and fine. Dolphins in schools. I took a small copper rod and soldered to it a barbed head cut from a piece of brass. This I set in a mop handle and attached a strong line. The first throw with this improvised spear struck a big dolphin, fully four feet long. After a struggle it was landed, when it thrashed about, tangling lines, and driving me out of the cockpit. I reached it with the knife, and as it died its color turned to the most brilliant silver, spotted with blue. Another was landed by its comrade where it lay yellow as gold with brown spots. I struck one through and through, but the barb did not hold. The wounded dolphin continued swimming alongside as if it was a common thing to have a harpoon drove home and pulled out.

Latitude at noon 5° 04' north.

Longitude 109° 30' west.

About this time a gannet took possession of the *Islander*. It first settled on the end of the mizzen boom, but not finding that perch satisfactory, tried the bowsprit, where it spent the afternoon preening its feathers and roosted there through the night like a chicken. The next morning it found a better place on the mizzen sheet outrigger, which place it came to regard as its own. A little later when we ran into a calm that set the *Islander* rolling and the sails to slatting and banging like mad, the bird was shaken off, but, as I could not fly, I had to stay. When a breeze steadied the ship once more, the gannet came back to its station.

Four days later another gannet joined us. As soon as it hove in sight the bird on the outrigger sat up and took notice. The newcomer circled about quite awhile before it decided to stop, then it came gliding in athwartship, striking me with its wing tip, and alighted on the upturned dinghy. After a glance at me it began in great haste to make up its toilet. There were several flies or bugs running in and out among its feathers that were causing it great annoyance, and it made every effort to scratch them off.

The bird's sanitary habits were not good, so I had to move it farther from the companionway. I had to use a stick, as it objected to being meddled with. I pushed it back off the dinghy though it resisted every inch. It tumbled into the cockpit and from there scrambled out on the deck aft, squawking and with feathers ruffled like a mad hen. When it went aft, the old bird on the outrigger ruffled up and came in to meet the intruder, who took up a fighting attitude. Beaks clashed, but the newcomer held its own, and the old bird went back to the outrigger fluttering and squawking.

The gannets were of different colors. The first appeared to be an old bird and was of a dull brown color with a bluish-black beak. The newcomer was brown above and white underneath, and had a greenish-yellow beak and feet. On account of their colors, I named one Blue Bill and the other Yellow Bill. They spent the greater part of their time preening their feathers, but went off several times a day for fish.

Blue Bill was very quarrelsome, and I kept a stick handy with which to join in when he made an attack on Yellow Bill. The birds always sighted a shark before I did, and I usually became aware of the presence of one of these scavengers through the actions of my feathered companions.

After running down the southeast trades until I went beyond the meridian of 110° west (a distance of some one thousand eight hundred miles to the westward of Panama) I stood off to northwest on a course to pass well to westward of Clipperton Island. This course soon brought us into the doldrums once more.

Monday, September 21.—Squall came up at 2 A.M. Wind and rain. Woke up to find the *Islander* tearing through a phosphorescent sea. Lowered the mains'l till the blow was over. Wind came from all around but finally settled down to south again. Rain and squalls at intervals until 3 P.M., when we ran out of it and wind fell light. Wind breezed up from south after sunset.

Tuesday, September 22.—Made a good run during the night and wind from south. Wind came round to southwest in the morning. The sea is full of fish and great numbers of birds are about. I tried for albacore, but a dolphin took the hook as it struck the water and made off faster than I could pay out line. It tore loose taking the hook along. When the bronze wire leader parted, the dolphin made the sea boil, shaking its head and lashing the water into foam with its struggles. It appeared to be trying to shake out the hook.

Latitude at noon 10° 27' north.

Longitude 113° 30' west.

Going north fast but a current is setting us to eastward of the course. During the afternoon I ran into a squall, and later a whirlwind came along. It was an incipient waterspout. The breeze was light, so that I had little more than steerageway on. I noticed it when about a mile away, as a dark column rising high in the air, similar to the column of dust and dirt carried upward by a whirlwind on land. When it was closer, I could see that it was composed of spray that was being whipped from the surface of the sea and whirled upward in the center of the disturbance. I watched it with interest until it was close up, and then I saw it was going to strike us fair. I jumped to the halyards and let the mains'l come down. For a moment the jib and mizzen snapped savagely, then it passed on to the northeast, still whirling up a column of spray.

When we entered the heat and damp of the doldrums once more, the fish that I had been trying to cure turned sour and spoiled, but this was of no consequence as there were always fresh ones to be had for the taking.

No part of the sea was so full of life as this. For more than a month a vast school of albacore and dolphins accompanied the *Islander* on her course. At night they appeared as great luminous wings stretching far on either side of the boat. In calm weather great numbers of turtles were seen floating lazily on the surface. There was a continuous flight of flying fishes striving to escape from the dolphins and albacore, often to be caught by the gannets and man-of-war birds that were always circling about.

According to the sailing directions, one might expect to pick up the northeast trade winds in the vicinity of Clipperton Island, but it was now the season when the trades are light in this region. I passed two degrees to the westward of Clipperton Island with no trade winds and still beat my slow way on into the northwest against contrary winds and squalls.

The barnacles were growing at an alarming rate and covered the rudder so completely that no part of the surface was to be seen. The *Islander* answered her helm about as well as a haystack would, and often when changing to the other tack, I had to wear her around. I made a scraper out of a block of hard wood and a bamboo pole, but at no time during my passage through the doldrums was the sea calm enough for me to go over the side after the barnacles. There certainly was a lack of wind, but the constantly recurring squalls kept up a continual jumble of cross seas. Progress under these circumstances was exasperatingly slow.

But it was not so monotonous as one might suppose. During the long passage through the doldrums, a day never passed without some excitement being occasioned by the squalls. The study of the weather, when one is depending on the wind, is a subject of never-ending interest, and one watches the approach of the last of a thousand rain squalls with as much interest as the first.

From the low-flying deck of the *Islander* I had a good opportunity to observe the fishes at close range, and there were few dull moments when watching them. One could scarce glance about without seeing a flying fish take to the air. With a voracious mouth snapping in close pursuit, the flying fish shoots up out of the water and glides down the wind until its momentum is gone, then often it skims the surface of a swell and gets in a few screwlike thrusts with its tail that sets it going again. But his peril is not over when he leaves the water. Often a dolphin tearing along in the water below is able to keep him in sight, and when the flying fish has exhausted his effort and tumbles in the water, the dolphin is right there to meet him. If a man-of-war bird or a gannet happens to be soaring near when he takes to the air, the bird swoops down and snaps him up in full flight.

One of the most startling sights that I saw was when a whole school of flying fishes, numbering thousands, took to the air, a gleaming silvery band spread out across the course of the *Islander*. Whether they were startled by my onrushing craft or were flying for the joy of it I could not tell, but they all left the water at the same time and at the end of the flight came down together.

I could have fared quite well on the flying fishes to be found lying about where they fell on deck after striking sails or rigging at night. As I lay in my berth I could hear them plump against the side of the cabin. In their frantic efforts to escape the rushes of the albacore and dolphins they often collided with the *Islander* in broad daylight, and I have been struck by them as I sat at the tiller. When one struck some part of the rigging and fell back into the water, there would be a violent commotion, as half a dozen albacore came together in a head-on collision in their rush to be first at the stunned flying fish.

I was dressing a large flying fish that had fallen on

deck with an idea of having a change from a steady diet of baked albacore. As a final touch I leaned over the side to wash it in the salt water, when an albacore darted from underneath and was off with my breakfast in a flash. I was only too glad that it did not take one of my fingers along as well.

One day I found a flying fish that had lodged under the dinghy and lain there till it was not so fresh as it might have been. I tossed it over the side, where a large fish of the tunny variety snapped it up and disappeared in the depth. A moment later the decayed flying fish came to the surface, having, no doubt, turned the stomach of a fish that takes its food alive and raw. A shark that was cruising beside the *Islander,* looking for just such dainties, now had a chance and slid leisurely up, rolled on his side, and took in the second-hand dinner. The difference in the manner in which the shark and the tunny took their meals was very noticeable. There was the trap-like snap of one compared to the leisurely movements of the other. I never saw a shark make a move toward an albacore, though it be swimming close by, and I believe he is too slow to take one unless it is disabled or dead. There is some mystery about the pilot fish, so often seen swimming just in front and above the shark's nose. It appears to me that it takes up this position as a safety measure. It is too quick for the shark, and at the same time, the predatory fishes hesitate when it comes to rushing in front of the mouth of so formidable a looking fish as the shark.

I offered Yellow Bill a flying fish that fell on deck. He took the fish from my hand, though he had some difficulty in swallowing it on account of the fins being dry. I tried Blue Bill with one, but the ill-natured bird only snapped viciously at me, knocking the fish out of my hand. However, there was no necessity for feeding the birds by hand. They seldom were away from the boat more than half an hour and then returned gorged to the last flying fish they could swallow.

After feeding, the care of their feathers was the most important business of the birds, and they spent hours on end oiling and preening them. Each wing feather was gone over separately, straightened out and laid down in perfect order. Oil was extracted from the oil gland and applied to the body feathers in just the right amount to make them waterproof. If they are to pursue and capture fish their flying equipment must be kept in perfect order, and this is a difficult task for a bird out at sea. Blue Bill and Yellow Bill must have taken quarters on the *Islander* in order to see to their toilet in comfort. I often passed flocks of gannets resting on the sea and caring for their feathers. They roll over so as to bring one side above the water, and after working on that for a time turn to the other side. Always one gannet seemed to be acting as sentinel while the rest were engaged in this task. At intervals of a few seconds he would thrust his head under water, from which position I presumed he could better detect the approach of a shark. Whenever the sentinel became alarmed, they all took to the air. In this region, I suppose a shark is the end of most good sea birds.

Down in this part of the ocean I met with a squid similar to the flying or leaping squid of the Indian Ocean, and often I would find more of these squid than flying fish on deck in the morning. The squid is an important part of the food of the dolphins and albacore, and when I threw overboard a squid that had ended its flight on deck, it caused a greater commotion among the albacore than a flying fish did. One evening a squid landed beside me in the cockpit. On deck it was entirely helpless and unable to move, but when I placed it in a basin of water it darted about furiously and ejected itself out on the deck again, leaving the water in the basin a murky brown color. The squid propels itself with a rocket-like movement by pumping a strong stream of water aft. When it is alarmed, it throws out a brown fluid with the stream, leaving a smoke screen behind to cover its retreat. At night the squid gave out a pale phosphorescent light.

I was having a rather interesting time with all this sea life, but, even so, I had no wish to linger in the heat and damp of the doldrums. On the evening of September 24th, after a night and day of squalls and rain I sailed abruptly out of it. Behind me the clouds hanging low over the sea had the appearance of steam rising from a caldron. Ahead was clear water and night came on with a starry sky.

Friday, September 25.—Ran all night with light west by north wind. Course north by west. Wind increasing during the morning and was blowing hard by noon. Lowered the mains'l while I had dinner and observed the sun for latitude.

Latitude at noon 12° 54′ north.

Longitude 114° west.

Tied two reefs in the main and carried on during the afternoon. Lay to under jib and mizzen after sunset.

The wind moderated during the night and came round to northwest, giving me several days of light head wind. Yellow Bill did not like it and headed off to the south. I never saw him again. I did not know of his intention to desert at the time, but Blue Bill did. As soon as he had gone, Blue Bill came in off his perch and took possession of the deck aft where he spent most of the day sleeping in the sun, quite content now that Yellow Bill had gone.

Friday, October 2.—Woke up at about 2 A.M. and found the wind howling out of north by west. Tied in a reef and stayed by the tiller till daylight, when there was a lull. Wind came round till we were headed west by south.

Latitude at noon 15° 31′ north.

Longitude 118° west.

During the afternoon the wind came round to west by south and we stood off to north by west. Hove to under jib and mizzen after sunset.

Saturday, October 3.—Wind moderate during the night and toward morning came round to west by south. Set the reefed mains'l at 4 A.M. Weather cleared during the morning.

Latitude at noon 15° 58′ north.

Longitude 118° 45' west.

Wind dying out during the afternoon. Light breeze after sunset. Could stand on the course to northwest all day.

Sunday, October 4.—Light fair wind during the night, but died out to a calm by noon.

Latitude at noon 16° 47' north.

Longitude 119° 30' west.

During the afternoon a squall came up from the south and blew strong with rain for an hour, after which wind fell to a calm. Sails slatting to drive one mad. After nightfall I took in the main.

Day after day I scanned the northeast horizon, hoping to see in the clouds some indication of relief from the conflicting winds against which the *Islander* was struggling, but the northeast trades were long in coming.

Tuesday, October 6.—Wind held on during the night. Light northeast wind blowing this morning. Looks like we had really run into the region of northeast winds. Tried for albacore, and hooked a large fish of unknown variety. When it found that something had hold of it, it streaked off, and I checked up so hard that we parted company. I hauled in the line to find the hook—a soft iron one, of Japanese make—straightened out. Tried again and caught an albacore for dinner.

Latitude at noon 17° 39' north.

Longitude 120° 30' west.

Beautiful day with light wind but stronger after sunset.

Wednesday, October 7.—Light northeast wind through the night. Wind increasing all morning.

Saw a drifting plank. Still vast numbers of albacore and flying fish.

Latitude at noon 18° 30′ north.

Longitude 121° 15′ west.

Tied two reefs in the mains'l at noon and one in the mizzen before sunset. To-day the *Islander* crossed the track she made when outward bound, November 28, 1921, and here completed the circumnavigation of the world.

There were a few days of rough going and then wind and sea moderated. As we passed out of the tropics the weather seemed cold and gloomy and there was scarce a bird to be seen. Blue Bill sat most of the time with his head under his wing. The weather did not suit him and the fishing was not good. After making the *Islander* his home for about a month, he went off one morning and did not return.

The wind continued light, and finding myself becalmed, I brought out the scraper I had made down in the doldrums. This was a block of hard wood to which was fixed a long bamboo handle. Launching the dinghy, to work from, I attacked the barnacles, which were now so thick on the *Islander's* bottom that there was no more standing room for them. From the dinghy I went after those growing under the bilges and on the keel where they could not be reached from the deck. From being long out of water, the dinghy leaked badly, and the rolling of the *Islander* on the swells made the work very difficult, but the scraper was very efficient, and tore the barnacles from their moorings in vast numbers. It was a great satisfaction to see them settling down into the pale blue depths of the sea. After a few hours of this, a breeze came up, and I had to cease operation and hoist in the dinghy. Two days later, when the wind fell light again, I dislodged what barnacles I could reach from the deck. The long bamboo handle of the scraper enabled me to get all that were in sight from the bow, and I was able to clear them entirely from the rudder. While I was engaged in this task, a few dolphins that had followed the *Islander* up from the doldrums became interested in the operation. When I struck a cluster of barnacles and dislodged them, the dolphins would rush to the spot to investigate and get a clout from the scraper. This only caused them to dart off a few feet and then they would come right back to see what had struck them. They were a most inquisitive lot of fishes.

In the end I had the barnacles pretty well cleared off, which improved the sailing qualities of the *Islander* greatly. If I had learned the knack of getting rid of these impediments earlier in the voyage, the run would have been shortened by many days.

About this time the sky became overcast with gray clouds passing at a very great height. The wind came round to south and then to the southwest. A long heavy swell set in with crests twelve seconds between. At the time, I was under the impression that a storm was in progress between my position and the coast. After two days the sky cleared and the wind came back to the northeast. When I arrived in California I learned that a severe hurricane had swept the Mexican shore.

At last the light fitful winds indicated that I had passed out of the limits of the trades, and I began to look for north or northwest winds. A few tropic birds hovered about for a time and then disappeared. Almost at the same time two albatross hove in sight.

Thursday, October 22.—Wind died out during the night. Took in the mains'l to stop the awful banging. Wind came up light and I put on the mains'l once more. Woke up before daylight and found the wind blowing fresh and strong from the north. Set a course northeast to bring up to the California coast. Had two reefs in the mains'l by noon. Sky overcast for the most part but there was a glimpse of the sun on the meridian.

Latitude at noon 30° 48′.

Longitude 127°.

Among the albacore swimming alongside is one that I have noticed for several days. It has a wound that is a great hole in its back. Wind slackened during the afternoon, but is blowing a good steady breeze after sunset.

Then followed some of the most beautiful days of the voyage. The wind was bracing but not cold. I saw kelp floating in the sea, and barnacle-covered pieces of wood. A gull came soaring by, and the albacore disappeared. There was a familiar haze in the air, and a land bird came to rest on the *Islander*. After flitting about the rigging for an hour or so it flew off to eastward.

Wednesday, October 28.—Fresh northwest wind during the night and to-day. Saw many gulls and pelicans, and drifting kelp. Sky overcast for the most part, but occasional glimpse of the sun.

Latitude at noon 33° 30'.

Longitude 120° 30'.

Set a course east northeast to bring up with San Nicholas Island.

During the night I kept a close lookout for San Nicholas Island, but the visibility was very poor. Morning came with clouds and haze, and no land had been sighted. I was wondering if my time had gone wrong or if my calculation was off. The wind was falling light, and I sailed slowly to eastward wishing for a sight of the sun when, just at noon, I sighted land on the starboard bow. It was the north end of San Clemente Island, and the first familiar land that I had sighted since I had taken departure from the south end of this same island almost four years before. San Nicholas was still in its proper position after all, but the weather had been too thick for me to see it. During the afternoon the breeze fell away to a calm, and the *Islander* drifted through the night while I slept. I turned out to the sound of a passing motorboat and found I had drifted under the lee of Catalina Island. In this familiar calm spot another day was passed before I had cleared the east end of the island and met the westerly breeze coming down the channel. Then the *Islander* glided into her home port as quietly as she had sailed away. At noon on October 31, 1925, her sails were furled in Los Angeles Harbor after completing a voyage around the world in three years eleven months and thirteen days.

Eighty-five days is a long time to be alone on the sea, but I bore it well. My health was better than when I sailed from Balboa. The whole voyage was carried out with less effort than I had anticipated. Only once did the *Islander* get in a position that required assistance to get her out, and she sustained no damages that I was not able to repair with my own resources. I never arrived in port complaining of hunger or a shortage of water. The *Islander* met some rough weather, but none that caused me any apprehension as to her seaworthiness.

I am often asked about how the *Islander* compares with other types of vessels. I have not had experience with other types, but I am of the opinion that I could have made the voyage in any well-found boat of the same size, but in none would it have been easier.

My voyage was not undertaken for the joy of sailing alone. It was my way of seeing some interesting parts of the world.

Ulysses is fabled to have had a very adventurous voyage while returning from the sack of Troy, but for sufficient reasons I avoided adventure as much as possible. Just the same, any landsman who builds his own vessel and sails it alone around the world will certainly meet with some adventures, so I shall offer no apology for my own voyage. Those days were the freest and happiest of my life. The *Islander* is seaworthy as ever, and the future may find her sailing over seas as beautiful as did the past.

THE END

A CATALOG OF SELECTED
DOVER BOOKS
IN ALL FIELDS OF INTEREST

A CATALOG OF SELECTED
DOVER BOOKS
IN ALL FIELDS OF INTEREST

DRAWINGS OF REMBRANDT, edited by Seymour Slive. Updated Lippmann, Hofstede de Groot edition, with definitive scholarly apparatus. All portraits, biblical sketches, landscapes, nudes. Oriental figures, classical studies, together with selection of work by followers. 550 illustrations. Total of 630pp. 9⅛ × 12¼.
21485-0, 21486-9 Pa., Two-vol. set $29.90

GHOST AND HORROR STORIES OF AMBROSE BIERCE, Ambrose Bierce. 24 tales vividly imagined, strangely prophetic, and decades ahead of their time in technical skill: "The Damned Thing," "An Inhabitant of Carcosa," "The Eyes of the Panther," "Moxon's Master," and 20 more. 199pp. 5⅜ × 8½. 20767-6 Pa. $4.95

ETHICAL WRITINGS OF MAIMONIDES, Maimonides. Most significant ethical works of great medieval sage, newly translated for utmost precision, readability. Laws Concerning Character Traits, Eight Chapters, more. 192pp. 5⅜ × 8½.
24522-5 Pa. $4.50

THE EXPLORATION OF THE COLORADO RIVER AND ITS CANYONS, J. W. Powell. Full text of Powell's 1,000-mile expedition down the fabled Colorado in 1869. Superb account of terrain, geology, vegetation, Indians, famine, mutiny, treacherous rapids, mighty canyons, during exploration of last unknown part of continental U.S. 400pp. 5⅜ × 8½. 20094-9 Pa. $7.95

HISTORY OF PHILOSOPHY, Julián Marías. Clearest one-volume history on the market. Every major philosopher and dozens of others, to Existentialism and later. 505pp. 5⅜ × 8½. 21739-6 Pa. $9.95

ALL ABOUT LIGHTNING, Martin A. Uman. Highly readable nontechnical survey of nature and causes of lightning, thunderstorms, ball lightning, St. Elmo's Fire, much more. Illustrated. 192pp. 5⅜ × 8½. 25237-X Pa. $5.95

SAILING ALONE AROUND THE WORLD, Captain Joshua Slocum. First man to sail around the world, alone, in small boat. One of great feats of seamanship told in delightful manner. 67 illustrations. 294pp. 5⅜ × 8½. 20326-3 Pa. $4.95

LETTERS AND NOTES ON THE MANNERS, CUSTOMS AND CONDITIONS OF THE NORTH AMERICAN INDIANS, George Catlin. Classic account of life among Plains Indians: ceremonies, hunt, warfare, etc. 312 plates. 572pp. of text. 6⅛ × 9¼. 22118-0, 22119-9, Pa., Two-vol. set $17.90

ALASKA: The Harriman Expedition, 1899, John Burroughs, John Muir, et al. Informative, engrossing accounts of two-month, 9,000-mile expedition. Native peoples, wildlife, forests, geography, salmon industry, glaciers, more. Profusely illustrated. 240 black-and-white line drawings. 124 black-and-white photographs. 3 maps. Index. 576pp. 5⅜ × 8½. 25109-8 Pa. $11.95

ILLUSTRATED DICTIONARY OF HISTORIC ARCHITECTURE, edited by Cyril M. Harris. Extraordinary compendium of clear, concise definitions for over 5,000 important architectural terms complemented by over 2,000 line drawings. Covers full spectrum of architecture from ancient ruins to 20th-century Modernism. Preface. 592pp. 7½ × 9⅝. 24444-X Pa. $15.95

THE NIGHT BEFORE CHRISTMAS, Clement C. Moore. Full text, and woodcuts from original 1848 book. Also critical, historical material. 19 illustrations. 40pp. 4⅝ × 6. 22797-9 Pa. $2.50

THE LESSON OF JAPANESE ARCHITECTURE: 165 Photographs, Jiro Harada. Memorable gallery of 165 photographs taken in the 1930s of exquisite Japanese homes of the well-to-do and historic buildings. 13 line diagrams. 192pp. 8⅜ × 11¼. 24778-3 Pa. $10.95

THE AUTOBIOGRAPHY OF CHARLES DARWIN AND SELECTED LETTERS, edited by Francis Darwin. The fascinating life of eccentric genius composed of an intimate memoir by Darwin (intended for his children); commentary by his son, Francis; hundreds of fragments from notebooks, journals, papers; and letters to and from Lyell, Hooker, Huxley, Wallace and Henslow. xi + 365pp. 5⅜ × 8. 20479-0 Pa. $6.95

WONDERS OF THE SKY: Observing Rainbows, Comets, Eclipses, the Stars and Other Phenomena, Fred Schaaf. Charming, easy-to-read poetic guide to all manner of celestial events visible to the naked eye. Mock suns, glories, Belt of Venus, more. Illustrated. 299pp. 5¼ × 8¼. 24402-4 Pa. $8.95

BURNHAM'S CELESTIAL HANDBOOK, Robert Burnham, Jr. Thorough guide to the stars beyond our solar system. Exhaustive treatment. Alphabetical by constellation: Andromeda to Cetus in Vol. 1; Chamaeleon to Orion in Vol. 2; and Pavo to Vulpecula in Vol. 3. Hundreds of illustrations. Index in Vol. 3. 2,000pp. 6⅛ × 9¼. 23567-X, 23568-8, 23673-0 Pa., Three-vol. set $41.85

STAR NAMES: Their Lore and Meaning, Richard Hinckley Allen. Fascinating history of names various cultures have given to constellations and literary and folkloristic uses that have been made of stars. Indexes to subjects. Arabic and Greek names. Biblical references. Bibliography. 563pp. 5⅜ × 8½. 21079-0 Pa. $8.95

THIRTY YEARS THAT SHOOK PHYSICS: The Story of Quantum Theory, George Gamow. Lucid, accessible introduction to influential theory of energy and matter. Careful explanations of Dirac's anti-particles, Bohr's model of the atom, much more. 12 plates. Numerous drawings. 240pp. 5⅜ × 8½. 24895-X Pa. $6.95

CHINESE DOMESTIC FURNITURE IN PHOTOGRAPHS AND MEASURED DRAWINGS, Gustav Ecke. A rare volume, now affordably priced for antique collectors, furniture buffs and art historians. Detailed review of styles ranging from early Shang to late Ming. Unabridged republication. 161 black-and-white drawings, photos. Total of 224pp. 8⅜ × 11¼. (Available in U.S. only) 25171-3 Pa. $14.95

VINCENT VAN GOGH: A Biography, Julius Meier-Graefe. Dynamic, penetrating study of artist's life, relationship with brother, Theo, painting techniques, travels, more. Readable, engrossing. 160pp. 5⅜ × 8½. (Available in U.S. only) 25253-1 Pa. $4.95

THE BLUE FAIRY BOOK, Andrew Lang. The first, most famous collection, with many familiar tales: Little Red Riding Hood, Aladdin and the Wonderful Lamp, Puss in Boots, Sleeping Beauty, Hansel and Gretel, Rumpelstiltskin; 37 in all. 138 illustrations. 390pp. 5⅜ × 8½. 21437-0 Pa. $6.95

THE STORY OF THE CHAMPIONS OF THE ROUND TABLE, Howard Pyle. Sir Launcelot, Sir Tristram and Sir Percival in spirited adventures of love and triumph retold in Pyle's inimitable style. 50 drawings, 31 full-page. xviii + 329pp. 6½ × 9¼. 21883-X Pa. $7.95

THE MYTHS OF THE NORTH AMERICAN INDIANS, Lewis Spence. Myths and legends of the Algonquins, Iroquois, Pawnees and Sioux with comprehensive historical and ethnological commentary. 36 illustrations. 5⅜ × 8½. 25967-6 Pa. $8.95

GREAT DINOSAUR HUNTERS AND THEIR DISCOVERIES, Edwin H. Colbert. Fascinating, lavishly illustrated chronicle of dinosaur research, 1820s to 1960. Achievements of Cope, Marsh, Brown, Buckland, Mantell, Huxley, many others. 384pp. 5¼ × 8¼. 24701-5 Pa. $7.95

THE TASTEMAKERS, Russell Lynes. Informal, illustrated social history of American taste 1850s–1950s. First popularized categories Highbrow, Lowbrow, Middlebrow. 129 illustrations. New (1979) afterword. 384pp. 6 × 9. 23993-4 Pa. $8.95

DOUBLE CROSS PURPOSES, Ronald A. Knox. A treasure hunt in the Scottish Highlands, an old map, unidentified corpse, surprise discoveries keep reader guessing in this cleverly intricate tale of financial skullduggery. 2 black-and-white maps. 320pp. 5⅜ × 8½. (Available in U.S. only) 25032-6 Pa. $6.95

AUTHENTIC VICTORIAN DECORATION AND ORNAMENTATION IN FULL COLOR: 46 Plates from "Studies in Design," Christopher Dresser. Superb full-color lithographs reproduced from rare original portfolio of a major Victorian designer. 48pp. 9¼ × 12¼. 25083-0 Pa. $7.95

PRIMITIVE ART, Franz Boas. Remains the best text ever prepared on subject, thoroughly discussing Indian, African, Asian, Australian, and, especially, Northern American primitive art. Over 950 illustrations show ceramics, masks, totem poles, weapons, textiles, paintings, much more. 376pp. 5⅜ × 8. 20025-6 Pa. $7.95

SIDELIGHTS ON RELATIVITY, Albert Einstein. Unabridged republication of two lectures delivered by the great physicist in 1920–21. *Ether and Relativity* and *Geometry and Experience*. Elegant ideas in nonmathematical form, accessible to intelligent layman. vi + 56pp. 5⅜ × 8½. 24511-X Pa. $3.95

THE WIT AND HUMOR OF OSCAR WILDE, edited by Alvin Redman. More than 1,000 ripostes, paradoxes, wisecracks: Work is the curse of the drinking classes, I can resist everything except temptation, etc. 258pp. 5⅜ × 8½. 20602-5 Pa. $4.95

ADVENTURES WITH A MICROSCOPE, Richard Headstrom. 59 adventures with clothing fibers, protozoa, ferns and lichens, roots and leaves, much more. 142 illustrations. 232pp. 5⅜ × 8½. 23471-1 Pa. $3.95

PLANTS OF THE BIBLE, Harold N. Moldenke and Alma L. Moldenke. Standard reference to all 230 plants mentioned in Scriptures. Latin name, biblical reference, uses, modern identity, much more. Unsurpassed encyclopedic resource for scholars, botanists, nature lovers, students of Bible. Bibliography. Indexes. 123 black-and-white illustrations. 384pp. 6 × 9. 25069-5 Pa. $8.95

FAMOUS AMERICAN WOMEN: A Biographical Dictionary from Colonial Times to the Present, Robert McHenry, ed. From Pocahontas to Rosa Parks, 1,035 distinguished American women documented in separate biographical entries. Accurate, up-to-date data, numerous categories, spans 400 years. Indices. 493pp. 6½ × 9¼. 24523-3 Pa. $10.95.

THE FABULOUS INTERIORS OF THE GREAT OCEAN LINERS IN HISTORIC PHOTOGRAPHS, William H. Miller, Jr. Some 200 superb photographs capture exquisite interiors of world's great "floating palaces"—1890s to 1980s: *Titanic, Ile de France, Queen Elizabeth, United States, Europa,* more. Approx. 200 black-and-white photographs. Captions. Text. Introduction. 160pp. 8⅞ × 11¾. 24756-2 Pa. $9.95

THE GREAT LUXURY LINERS, 1927-1954: A Photographic Record, William H. Miller, Jr. Nostalgic tribute to heyday of ocean liners. 186 photos of *Ile de France, Normandie, Leviathan, Queen Elizabeth, United States,* many others. Interior and exterior views. Introduction. Captions. 160pp. 9 × 12. 24056-8 Pa. $10.95

A NATURAL HISTORY OF THE DUCKS, John Charles Phillips. Great landmark of ornithology offers complete detailed coverage of nearly 200 species and subspecies of ducks: gadwall, sheldrake, merganser, pintail, many more. 74 full-color plates, 102 black-and-white. Bibliography. Total of 1,920pp. 8⅜ × 11¼. 25141-1, 25142-X Cloth., Two-vol. set $100.00

THE SEAWEED HANDBOOK: An Illustrated Guide to Seaweeds from North Carolina to Canada, Thomas F. Lee. Concise reference covers 78 species. Scientific and common names, habitat, distribution, more. Finding keys for easy identification. 224pp. 5⅜ × 8½. 25215-9 Pa. $6.95

THE TEN BOOKS OF ARCHITECTURE: The 1755 Leoni Edition, Leon Battista Alberti. Rare classic helped introduce the glories of ancient architecture to the Renaissance. 68 black-and-white plates. 336pp. 8⅜ × 11¼. 25239-6 Pa. $14.95

MISS MACKENZIE, Anthony Trollope. Minor masterpieces by Victorian master unmasks many truths about life in 19th-century England. First inexpensive edition in years. 392pp. 5⅜ × 8½. 25201-9 Pa. $8.95

THE RIME OF THE ANCIENT MARINER, Gustave Doré, Samuel Taylor Coleridge. Dramatic engravings considered by many to be his greatest work. The terrifying space of the open sea, the storms and whirlpools of an unknown ocean, the ice of Antarctica, more—all rendered in a powerful, chilling manner. Full text. 38 plates. 77pp. 9¼ × 12. 22305-1 Pa. $4.95

THE EXPEDITIONS OF ZEBULON MONTGOMERY PIKE, Zebulon Montgomery Pike. Fascinating firsthand accounts (1805-6) of exploration of Mississippi River, Indian wars, capture by Spanish dragoons, much more. 1,088pp. 5⅜ × 8½. 25254-X, 25255-8 Pa., Two-vol. set $25.90

SIR HARRY HOTSPUR OF HUMBLETHWAITE, Anthony Trollope. Incisive, unconventional psychological study of a conflict between a wealthy baronet, his idealistic daughter, and their scapegrace cousin. The 1870 novel in its first inexpensive edition in years. 250pp. 5⅜ × 8½. 24953-0 Pa. $6.95

LASERS AND HOLOGRAPHY, Winston E. Kock. Sound introduction to burgeoning field, expanded (1981) for second edition. Wave patterns, coherence, lasers, diffraction, zone plates, properties of holograms, recent advances. 84 illustrations. 160pp. 5⅜ × 8¼. (Except in United Kingdom) 24041-X Pa. $3.95

INTRODUCTION TO ARTIFICIAL INTELLIGENCE: Second, Enlarged Edition, Philip C. Jackson, Jr. Comprehensive survey of artificial intelligence—the study of how machines (computers) can be made to act intelligently. Includes introductory and advanced material. Extensive notes updating the main text. 132 black-and-white illustrations. 512pp. 5⅜ × 8½. 24864-X Pa. $10.95

HISTORY OF INDIAN AND INDONESIAN ART, Ananda K. Coomaraswamy. Over 400 illustrations illuminate classic study of Indian art from earliest Harappa finds to early 20th century. Provides philosophical, religious and social insights. 304pp. 6⅜ × 9⅜. 25005-9 Pa. $11.95

THE GOLEM, Gustav Meyrink. Most famous supernatural novel in modern European literature, set in Ghetto of Old Prague around 1890. Compelling story of mystical experiences, strange transformations, profound terror. 13 black-and-white illustrations. 224pp. 5⅜ × 8½. (Available in U.S. only) 25025-3 Pa. $6.95

PICTORIAL ENCYCLOPEDIA OF HISTORIC ARCHITECTURAL PLANS, DETAILS AND ELEMENTS: With 1,880 Line Drawings of Arches, Domes, Doorways, Facades, Gables, Windows, etc., John Theodore Haneman. Sourcebook of inspiration for architects, designers, others. Bibliography. Captions. 141pp. 9 × 12. 24605-1 Pa. $7.95

BENCHLEY LOST AND FOUND, Robert Benchley. Finest humor from early 30s, about pet peeves, child psychologists, post office and others. Mostly unavailable elsewhere. 73 illustrations by Peter Arno and others. 183pp. 5⅜ × 8½. 22410-4 Pa. $4.95

ERTÉ GRAPHICS, Erté. Collection of striking color graphics: *Seasons, Alphabet, Numerals, Aces* and *Precious Stones.* 50 plates, including 4 on covers. 48pp. 9⅜ × 12¼. 23580-7 Pa. $7.95

THE JOURNAL OF HENRY D. THOREAU, edited by Bradford Torrey, F. H. Allen. Complete reprinting of 14 volumes, 1837–61, over two million words; the sourcebooks for *Walden*, etc. Definitive. All original sketches, plus 75 photographs. 1,804pp. 8½ × 12¼. 20312-3, 20313-1 Cloth., Two-vol. set $130.00

CASTLES: Their Construction and History, Sidney Toy. Traces castle development from ancient roots. Nearly 200 photographs and drawings illustrate moats, keeps, baileys, many other features. Caernarvon, Dover Castles, Hadrian's Wall, Tower of London, dozens more. 256pp. 5⅜ × 8¼. 24898-4 Pa. $6.95

AMERICAN CLIPPER SHIPS: 1833–1858, Octavius T. Howe & Frederick C. Matthews. Fully-illustrated, encyclopedic review of 352 clipper ships from the period of America's greatest maritime supremacy. Introduction. 109 halftones. 5 black-and-white line illustrations. Index. Total of 928pp. 5⅜ × 8½.
25115-2, 25116-0 Pa., Two-vol. set $17.90

TOWARDS A NEW ARCHITECTURE, Le Corbusier. Pioneering manifesto by great architect, near legendary founder of "International School." Technical and aesthetic theories, views on industry, economics, relation of form to function, "mass-production spirit," much more. Profusely illustrated. Unabridged translation of 13th French edition. Introduction by Frederick Etchells. 320pp. 6⅛ × 9¼. (Available in U.S. only)
25023-7 Pa. $8.95

THE BOOK OF KELLS, edited by Blanche Cirker. Inexpensive collection of 32 full-color, full-page plates from the greatest illuminated manuscript of the Middle Ages, painstakingly reproduced from rare facsimile edition. Publisher's Note. Captions. 32pp. 9⅜ × 12¼.
24345-1 Pa. $5.95

BEST SCIENCE FICTION STORIES OF H. G. WELLS, H. G. Wells. Full novel *The Invisible Man*, plus 17 short stories: "The Crystal Egg," "Aepyornis Island," "The Strange Orchid," etc. 303pp. 5⅜ × 8½. (Available in U.S. only)
21531-8 Pa. $6.95

AMERICAN SAILING SHIPS: Their Plans and History, Charles G. Davis. Photos, construction details of schooners, frigates, clippers, other sailcraft of 18th to early 20th centuries—plus entertaining discourse on design, rigging, nautical lore, much more. 137 black-and-white illustrations. 240pp. 6⅛ × 9¼.
24658-2 Pa. $6.95

ENTERTAINING MATHEMATICAL PUZZLES, Martin Gardner. Selection of author's favorite conundrums involving arithmetic, money, speed, etc., with lively commentary. Complete solutions. 112pp. 5⅜ × 8½.   25211-6 Pa. $3.50

THE WILL TO BELIEVE, HUMAN IMMORTALITY, William James. Two books bound together. Effect of irrational on logical, and arguments for human immortality. 402pp. 5⅜ × 8½.   20291-7 Pa. $8.95

THE HAUNTED MONASTERY and THE CHINESE MAZE MURDERS, Robert Van Gulik. 2 full novels by Van Gulik continue adventures of Judge Dee and his companions. An evil Taoist monastery, seemingly supernatural events; overgrown topiary maze that hides strange crimes. Set in 7th-century China. 27 illustrations. 328pp. 5⅜ × 8½.   23502-5 Pa. $6.95

CELEBRATED CASES OF JUDGE DEE (DEE GOONG AN), translated by Robert Van Gulik. Authentic 18th-century Chinese detective novel; Dee and associates solve three interlocked cases. Led to Van Gulik's own stories with same characters. Extensive introduction. 9 illustrations. 237pp. 5⅜ × 8½.
23337-5 Pa. $5.95

Prices subject to change without notice.

Available at your book dealer or write for free catalog to Dept. GI, Dover Publications, Inc., 31 East 2nd St., Mineola, N.Y. 11501. Dover publishes more than 175 books each year on science, elementary and advanced mathematics, biology, music, art, literary history, social sciences and other areas.